SCANDINAVIA TRAVEL GUIDE 2023

An Unforgettable Journey through Denmark, Iceland, Finland And Sweden Stunning Landscapes and Rich Culture

LINDA J. MOORE

D1241758

Table Of Contents

Welcome to Scandinavia

I had always been fascinated by the Nordic countries and their distinct culture, and I was finally able to see it for myself. As I walked around the vibrant streets of Copenhagen, Denmark, I felt the energy of the city. The vibrant buildings, charming canals, and delectable food all made an impression on me.

I spent a few days in Copenhagen, visiting famous landmarks such as the Little Mermaid statue and the Tivoli Gardens. I also took a boat tour of the city's canals, which was an excellent way to see the city from a new angle. The tour was extremely knowledgeable and shared fascinating stories and facts about the history of the city.

Following my time in Copenhagen, I boarded a train to Stockholm, Sweden. The train ride was beautiful, passing through lush green forests and small towns. When I first arrived in Stockholm, I was struck by its beauty. The architecture was stunning, and the streets were lined with brightly colored structures and charming shops. I also went to the Vasa Museum, which houses an impressive 17th century warship recovered from the sea.

I took a ferry from Stockholm to Helsinki, Finland. The ferry ride was pleasant and relaxing, and I appreciated the beautiful views of the Baltic Sea. Helsinki was an entirely different experience than the other cities I'd visited thus far. With sleek skyscrapers and trendy cafes, it had a more modern and cosmopolitan feel. I went to the Suomenlinna fortress, a UNESCO World Heritage site with stunning views of the city and the sea.

Finally, I arrived in Norway, my favorite country of the journey. I arrived in Oslo and immediately felt the city's energy. It was crowded, and the streets were lined with street performers and vendors. I went to the Viking Ship Museum, which houses three well-preserved 9th-century Viking ships. It was fascinating to see these ancient ships up close and learn about Viking history.

The Northern Lights, however, were the highlight of my trip. I'd always wanted to see them, and I was fortunate enough to see them on my final night in Norway. I took a bus tour outside of town, and we arrived at a remote location in the middle of nowhere. We huddled around a campfire and shared stories with the other tourists while we waited for the lights to appear. The sky was suddenly filled with dancing green and purple lights, as if by magic. It was an unforgettable experience that I will remember for the rest of my life.

I couldn't wait to tell my friends and family about my adventures when I got home. I showed them all of my photos and told them about the various places I visited and sights I saw. I also made a point of recommending my favorite spots, and I even gave them a list of must-see attractions and the best restaurants I'd visited.

My friends and family were so taken with my trip that they asked me to organize one for them. I was glad to do it, and I enjoyed researching the various places and activities that they might enjoy. I even assisted them in booking their flights and lodging. It was a fantastic experience to feel like a travel agent.

Since my trip to Scandinavia, I've developed a greater appreciation for the Nordic countries' culture and history. I also made some wonderful memories and met some amazing people. I'm already planning my next trip to Scandinavia, this time to Iceland; I've heard it's one of the most beautiful places on the planet, and I can't wait to see it for myself.

My trip to Scandinavia was an unforgettable experience, and I am grateful for the chance to see such beautiful places and meet such wonderful people. I'm excited to keep exploring and learning about the world and the various cultures that make it such an interesting place.

CHAPTER 1

INTRODUCTION

Brief History

Scandinavia is a region located in Northern Europe, consisting of Denmark, Norway, and Sweden. It has a rich history that dates back to the prehistoric times. The Scandinavian people have left their mark on the world in various fields such as literature, music, art, and technology. In this essay, we will take a brief look at the history of Scandinavia, from its earliest settlements to modern times.

- **Prehistoric Scandinavia**

The earliest evidence of human settlement in Scandinavia dates back to around 12,000 BCE. During this time, the region was covered by ice, and the first inhabitants were hunters and gatherers who lived in small groups. As the ice began to recede, the climate became milder, and people began to settle in larger communities. Archaeological evidence from this period shows that the people of Scandinavia were skilled at fishing and hunting and had developed a sophisticated culture.

- **Bronze Age Scandinavia**

Around 1800 BCE, the people of Scandinavia began to use bronze for tools and weapons. This period is known as the Bronze Age. During this time, the people of Scandinavia developed a complex society with large farms, longhouses, and trade networks. The bronze age also saw the development of religious practices, with the worship of the sun and the moon being prominent. The famous Bronze Age rock carvings, which can still be seen today, depict scenes from everyday life, as well as animals, boats, and weapons.

- **Iron Age Scandinavia**

The Iron Age in Scandinavia began around 500 BCE and lasted until the Viking Age. During this time, iron replaced bronze as the primary material for tools and weapons. The Iron Age saw the emergence of the Germanic peoples in Scandinavia, who were known for their warlike nature and their love of poetry and storytelling. The Iron Age also saw the spread of Christianity in Scandinavia, with the first Christian churches being built in the region.

- **Viking Age Scandinavia**

The Viking Age in Scandinavia began in the late 8th century and lasted until the 11th century. The Vikings were known for their seafaring abilities, and they traveled throughout Europe, Asia, and even North America. The Vikings were feared and respected for their military prowess, and their reputation as raiders and conquerors has lasted to this day.

The Vikings left behind a rich legacy of art, literature, and technology. They were skilled at shipbuilding, and their longships were renowned for their speed and maneuverability. The Vikings also developed a system of writing, known as runes, which they used for both magical and practical purposes. The Viking Age also saw the emergence of great poets and storytellers, who passed down their stories from generation to generation.

● **Medieval Scandinavia**

After the Viking Age, Scandinavia entered a period of relative peace and stability. The region was ruled by a series of powerful kings, who were able to unite the disparate tribes and clans under their rule. During the Middle Ages, Scandinavia became a center of trade and commerce, with cities such as Bergen, Stockholm, and Copenhagen emerging as important trading hubs.

The Middle Ages also saw the spread of Christianity throughout Scandinavia. The Christianization of the region was a gradual process, but by the end of the Middle Ages, Christianity had become the dominant religion in Scandinavia. The region also saw the emergence of great architects, such as the Danish architect

Esbern Snare, who designed many of the great Gothic cathedrals that still stand today.

Modern Scandinavia

In the 19th and 20th centuries, Scandinavia underwent significant social and political changes. The region saw the emergence of strong labor movements, which led to the development of the welfare state. Today, the Scandinavian countries are known for their high levels of social equality, universal healthcare, and free education.

During the 20th century, the Scandinavian countries also played important roles in world affairs. Sweden was neutral during World War II but provided aid to the Allied powers. After the war, Sweden became a leader in international diplomacy and played an important role in the formation of the United Nations.

Denmark, Norway, and Sweden have all played important roles in the development of modern technology. Sweden, in particular, is known for its contributions to the field of telecommunications, with companies like Ericsson leading the way in mobile technology. Denmark is known for its design and architecture, with iconic buildings such as the Sydney Opera House and the Guggenheim Museum Bilbao being designed by Danish architects.

Norway is known for its expertise in oil and gas exploration, with companies such as Statoil being leaders in the field.

Today, Scandinavia is a prosperous and peaceful region with a rich cultural heritage. The people of Scandinavia continue to be leaders in the fields of science, technology, and the arts. The region is also known for its commitment to social equality, with policies that ensure that everyone has access to education, healthcare, and social services.

Scandinavia Weather

- **Winter**

Winter in Scandinavia is long and can be very cold. Temperatures in the northern parts of the region can drop as low as -40 degrees Celsius, while the milder southern regions experience temperatures of around -5 degrees Celsius. Snow is common in most parts of Scandinavia, with the northern regions receiving the most snowfall. The snow is often heavy and can cause disruptions to transportation and daily life. However, the snow also provides opportunities for winter sports, such as skiing, snowboarding, and ice skating.

One of the most significant weather phenomena during the winter in Scandinavia is the polar night. In the northernmost parts of

Scandinavia, the sun does not rise above the horizon for several weeks during the winter months. This can have a significant impact on the daily life and mental health of the people living in these areas. However, the polar night also provides a unique opportunity to witness the aurora borealis, also known as the Northern Lights.

1. Spring

Spring in Scandinavia is a time of transition. The snow begins to melt, and the days become longer. However, the weather can still be unpredictable, with periods of rain and snow followed by sunny days. The temperature slowly starts to rise, and by the end of spring, the days can be warm and pleasant.

One of the most beautiful phenomena during the spring in Scandinavia is the blooming of wildflowers. The region is home to several species of wildflowers, and the fields and meadows burst into a riot of colors during the spring months. This is a popular time for hiking and exploring the countryside.

● Summer

Summer in Scandinavia is a time of long days and mild temperatures. The sun shines for almost 24 hours a day in the northern parts of the region, and the days are filled with outdoor activities such as hiking, swimming, and fishing. The temperature can vary depending on the location, with the southern parts of

Scandinavia experiencing temperatures of around 20-25 degrees Celsius, while the northern parts have temperatures of around 10-15 degrees Celsius.

One of the most significant weather phenomena during the summer in Scandinavia is the midnight sun. In the northernmost parts of the region, the sun does not set for several weeks during the summer months. This provides a unique opportunity to enjoy the outdoors at all hours of the day and night.

● **Autumn**

Autumn in Scandinavia is a time of changing colors and crisp temperatures. The leaves on the trees turn a riot of red, orange, and gold, and the forests are filled with the sound of rustling leaves. The temperature begins to drop, and the days become shorter. The weather can be unpredictable, with periods of sunny days followed by rain and wind.

One of the most significant weather phenomena during the autumn in Scandinavia is the Northern Lights. As the nights become longer and darker, the aurora borealis becomes more visible, providing a spectacular display of colors in the night sky.

Best Time to Visit

Deciding on the best time to visit Scandinavia depends on what you want to do and see. Each season offers its own unique experiences and weather conditions, so it is important to consider your preferences and interests before planning your trip. In this essay, we will take a closer look at the best times to visit Scandinavia based on different factors.

Summer (June-August)

Summer is the most popular time to visit Scandinavia, and for good reason. The weather is mild, with temperatures ranging from 15-25 degrees Celsius. The days are long, with almost 24 hours of daylight in the northern parts of the region. This makes it the perfect time for outdoor activities such as hiking, biking, swimming, and fishing. The summer months are also the best time to explore the region's beautiful cities and towns, with many festivals and cultural events taking place.

One of the most popular summer events in Scandinavia is the Midsummer celebrations. This is a traditional holiday that takes place in late June and is celebrated with music, dancing, and food. The celebrations are especially lively in Sweden, where people gather around maypoles to sing and dance.

Autumn (September-November)

Autumn in Scandinavia is a beautiful season, with the trees changing color and the air becoming crisp. The weather can be unpredictable, with periods of rain and wind, but there are also many sunny days. Autumn is a great time to explore the countryside, with many hiking trails and scenic drives offering stunning views of the changing colors.

One of the most significant events during the autumn in Scandinavia is the Northern Lights. As the nights become longer and darker, the aurora borealis becomes more visible, providing a spectacular display of colors in the night sky. The best time to see the Northern Lights is from September to March, with the peak season being in December and January.

Winter (December-February)

Winter in Scandinavia is long and can be very cold, but it also offers some unique experiences that are not available during the other seasons. The snow provides opportunities for winter sports such as skiing, snowboarding, and ice skating. The polar night, which occurs in the northernmost parts of the region, provides a unique opportunity to witness the aurora borealis.

One of the most significant winter events in Scandinavia is Christmas. The region is known for its Christmas markets and traditions, with cities and towns offering festive decorations, music, and food. Many cities also have ice-skating rinks and other winter activities during the Christmas season.

Spring (March-May)

Spring in Scandinavia is a time of transition, with the snow melting and the days becoming longer. The weather can still be unpredictable, with periods of rain and snow followed by sunny days. Spring is a great time to explore the countryside and see the blooming of wildflowers.

One of the most significant events during the spring in Scandinavia is Easter. The region has many Easter traditions, including the decorating of Easter trees and the consumption of traditional Easter foods such as eggs and herring.

How To Get There

Flying to Scandinavia

Flying to Scandinavia is the most common way to get there, and there are several airports to choose from, depending on your destination. The three main airports in Scandinavia are Oslo Airport (OSL) in Norway, Stockholm Arlanda Airport (ARN) in

Sweden, and Copenhagen Airport (CPH) in Denmark. These airports are well-connected to major cities around the world, and you can easily find direct flights from most major cities in Europe, North America, and Asia.

There are many airlines that fly to Scandinavia, including major carriers such as Scandinavian Airlines (SAS), Norwegian, Finnair, Lufthansa, and British Airways, among others. Prices for flights to Scandinavia can vary depending on the season, time of day, and how far in advance you book your tickets. If you are flexible with your travel dates, you may be able to find cheaper flights. It's also worth checking different airlines to compare prices.

If you are traveling from within Europe, you may be able to find budget airlines such as Ryanair, EasyJet, and Wizz Air, which offer cheaper flights to Scandinavia. However, be aware that these airlines may charge extra fees for baggage and other services, so be sure to read the fine print before booking.

Getting to Scandinavia by Train

If you are traveling from within Europe, you may also consider taking the train to Scandinavia. There are several train routes that connect Scandinavia to other parts of Europe, including the famous Oslo to Bergen Railway, which is considered one of the most scenic train rides in the world. The route takes you through Norway's stunning fjord landscapes, and it's a great way to see the country's natural beauty up close.

Other popular train routes include the Stockholm to Oslo train, the Copenhagen to Stockholm train, and the Helsinki to St. Petersburg train. These routes are operated by different train companies, including SJ in Sweden, Vy in Norway, and VR in Finland. You can book train tickets online, and prices vary depending on the season and how far in advance you book.

Getting to Scandinavia by Ferry

Another option for getting to Scandinavia is by taking a ferry. There are several ferry companies that operate routes between Scandinavia and other parts of Europe, including Stena Line, DFDS Seaways, and Tallink Silja Line, among others.

Ferries are a great option if you are traveling with a car, as you can take your vehicle on board and explore Scandinavia at your own pace. Some of the most popular ferry routes include the Copenhagen to Oslo ferry, the Helsinki to Stockholm ferry, and the Tallinn to Helsinki ferry.

Prices for ferry tickets vary depending on the season and how far in advance you book. You can book ferry tickets online, and some companies offer discounts if you book return tickets or if you are traveling with children.

Getting Around Scandinavia

Once you arrive in Scandinavia, there are several options for getting around, including trains, buses, and rental cars. Scandinavia has an excellent public transportation system, and it's easy to get around by train or bus. In Norway and Sweden, you can buy a rail pass that allows you to travel on all trains and buses within the country, making it a cost-effective way to see the sights.

If you prefer to have more freedom and flexibility, renting a car is also a good option. You can easily rent a car at the airport or in major cities, and the roads in Scandinavia are well-maintained and easy to navigate. However, keep in mind that driving in winter can be challenging due to snow and icy roads, so it's important to check the weather forecast and drive carefully.

It's also worth noting that there are several low-cost airlines operating within Scandinavia, including Norwegian and SAS. These airlines offer cheap flights to smaller cities within the region, making it easy to explore different parts of Scandinavia. You can also take a domestic flight to the remote regions of Norway, such as the Arctic Circle or the Lofoten Islands.

Finally, Scandinavia is known for its extensive network of hiking and cycling trails, making it a popular destination for outdoor enthusiasts. There are several d tours available, or you can rent a bike and explore the countryside on your own. It's important to bring appropriate clothing and gear, especially if you are planning to hike or cycle in remote areas.

15 Reasons To Plan a Trip To Scandinavia As Your Next Vacation Destination

- **Natural Beauty:** Scandinavia is known for its stunning natural landscapes, from Norway's fjords to Sweden's forests and Finland's lakes.
- **Northern Lights:** Scandinavia is one of the best places in the world to see the Northern Lights, a stunning natural phenomenon.
- **Outdoor Activities:** Scandinavia is a great destination for outdoor activities, including hiking, cycling, skiing, and fishing.
- **Rich Culture:** Scandinavia has a rich cultural heritage, with a long history of art, literature, and music.

- **Modern Architecture:** Scandinavia is home to some of the most innovative and modern architecture in the world, such as the Oresund Bridge and the Oslo Opera House.

- **Delicious Cuisine:** Scandinavian cuisine is known for its fresh seafood, game meats, and delicious pastries.

- **Sustainable Travel:** Scandinavia is a leader in sustainable travel, with a focus on eco-friendly accommodations and activities.

- **Safe and Welcoming:** Scandinavia is known for its safe and welcoming atmosphere, making it a great destination for solo travelers and families.

- **Outdoor Saunas:** Scandinavia is famous for its outdoor saunas, a traditional way to relax and unwind after a day of activities.

- **Midnight Sun:** During the summer months, Scandinavia experiences the Midnight Sun, where the sun never fully sets, providing 24-hour daylight.

- **Hygge:** The Danish concept of "hygge" is all about coziness and enjoying life's simple pleasures, making it a great way to relax and unwind.

- **Viking History:** Scandinavia has a rich history of Vikings, and there are many museums and historical sites dedicated to this fascinating culture.

- **Wildlife:** Scandinavia is home to a wide variety of wildlife, including reindeer, elk, wolves, and polar bears.
- **Design:** Scandinavia is known for its clean, minimalist design, which can be seen in everything from furniture to fashion.
- **Christmas Markets:** Scandinavia is home to some of the best Christmas markets in the world, with festive decorations, delicious food, and unique gifts.

CHAPTER 2

TIPS AND CONSIDERATIONS

Visiting Scandinavia on a Budget

- **Transportation**

Getting around in Scandinavia can be expensive, but there are some ways to save money. First, consider purchasing a regional rail pass or bus pass, which can provide significant savings compared to buying individual tickets. Also, be flexible with your travel dates and times, as off-peak travel can be much cheaper. Additionally, consider using public transportation instead of taxis or private cars, which can be much more expensive.

- **Accommodation**

Accommodation in Scandinavia can be costly, but there are several ways to reduce costs. One option is to stay in hostels, which are relatively affordable and offer a chance to meet fellow travelers. Additionally, many Scandinavian cities have Airbnb rentals, which can provide a more local experience while also being less expensive than hotels. Finally, consider camping, especially in the summer months when the weather is mild. There are many campgrounds throughout Scandinavia, and camping can be a great way to experience the natural beauty of the region.

- **Food and Drink**

Food and drink costs can add up quickly in Scandinavia, but there are ways to save money while still enjoying the local cuisine. One option is to cook your meals, either in a hostel or Airbnb kitchen or by camping and bringing your own camping stove. This can be a great way to save money while also experiencing the local markets and food culture. Additionally, many Scandinavian cities have food trucks and street vendors that offer affordable and delicious meals. Finally, consider drinking tap water instead of buying bottled water, as the tap water in Scandinavia is safe to drink and is often of high quality.

- **Sightseeing**

Sightseeing in Scandinavia can be expensive, but there are several ways to save money while still experiencing the region's attractions. First, consider visiting museums and other attractions during their free or discounted hours. Many museums and other cultural institutions offer free or reduced admission on certain days or during certain times, so do some research before you go. Additionally, consider taking advantage of the many outdoor activities that Scandinavia has to offer, such as hiking, biking, and skiing. These activities are often free or low-cost and can provide a unique perspective on the natural beauty of the region.

Miscellaneous Expenses

Finally, there are some miscellaneous expenses to consider when visiting Scandinavia. One of these is the cost of internet and mobile phone service, which can be quite high. To save money, consider using free Wi-Fi when available or purchasing a local SIM card for your phone. Additionally, be aware of the high taxes on goods and services in Scandinavia, which can add significant costs to purchases. Finally, consider packing light to avoid baggage fees on airlines and trains, which can be quite expensive.

Expenses

To provide an idea of the expenses of traveling to Scandinavia on a budget, we have put together a sample itinerary for a 10-day trip to Norway, Sweden, and Denmark. This itinerary includes transportation, accommodation, food, and sightseeing costs, but does not include miscellaneous expenses such as internet and phone service.

Transportation:

- Round-trip flight from New York to Oslo: $400
- Regional rail pass for 3 countries: $250
- Local transportation (buses and subways): $50

Accommodation:

- 3 nights in Oslo hostel: $120
- 3 nights in Stockholm Airbnb: $180
- 3 nights in Copenhagen campground: $90

Food and Drink:

- Groceries for 3&7 days (cooking some meals, eating out other meals): $200
- Street food and snacks: $100

Sightseeing:

- Oslo Pass (includes free admission to museums and public transportation): $80
- Stockholm Pass (includes free admission to museums and public transportation): $80
- Copenhagen Card (includes free admission to museums and public transportation): $80

Total Expenses: $1,380

Of course, these costs are just estimates and will vary depending on your travel style and preferences. However, this sample itinerary provides an idea of how it is possible to explore Scandinavia on a budget without sacrificing too much comfort or experience.

Getting Around Scandinavia

By Train

One of the best ways to explore Scandinavia is by train. Trains are a comfortable and convenient mode of transportation that offer some of the most spectacular views of the region's stunning landscapes. In addition, trains are often faster and more efficient than other modes of transportation, such as buses or ferries.

If you are planning to travel by train in Scandinavia, there are several options available to you. One of the most popular is the Eurail Scandinavia Pass, which allows you to travel throughout the region for a set period of time. This pass is ideal for travelers who want to explore multiple destinations in Scandinavia, as it allows you to hop on and off trains at your leisure.

Another option is to purchase individual tickets for each leg of your journey. While this may be more expensive than the Eurail pass, it can be a more flexible option for travelers who are only planning to visit a few destinations.

By Bus

Buses are another popular mode of transportation in Scandinavia, and they are often more affordable than trains. However, they can be slower and less comfortable than trains, especially for long journeys.

One of the best ways to save money on bus travel in Scandinavia is to book in advance. Many bus companies offer early bird discounts, which can save you a significant amount of money on your journey. Additionally, some bus companies offer student discounts or other special promotions that can help you save even more.

By Car

If you prefer to have more freedom and flexibility during your travels, renting a car may be the best option for you. While renting a car can be more expensive than other modes of transportation, it allows you to explore the region at your own pace and visit more remote locations that may not be accessible by public transportation.

If you decide to rent a car in Scandinavia, be sure to shop around for the best deals. Many car rental companies offer discounts for longer rental periods or for booking in advance. Additionally, be aware that driving in Scandinavia can be quite different from driving in other parts of the world, so be sure to familiarize yourself with the local traffic laws and road signs.

By Ferry

Scandinavia is surrounded by water, which means that ferries are an important mode of transportation in the region. Ferries are often used to travel between islands or to connect the mainland with more remote areas.

If you are planning to travel by ferry in Scandinavia, be sure to check the schedules and book in advance, especially during peak travel season. Additionally, many ferry companies offer discounts for booking in advance or for purchasing round-trip tickets.

By Bike

If you are looking for a more active and eco-friendly way to explore Scandinavia, cycling may be the perfect option for you. Scandinavia is known for its stunning bike routes, which offer some of the most breathtaking views of the region's natural landscapes.

If you decide to travel by bike in Scandinavia, be sure to bring all the necessary gear, including a helmet, bike lock, and repair kit. Additionally, be aware of the local traffic laws and road conditions, and be sure to plan your route carefully.

Shopping in Scandinavia

Copenhagen, Denmark

Copenhagen is known for its sleek and stylish design, and it is a great place to shop for high-quality Scandinavian fashion and homeware. Some of the best places to shop in Copenhagen include the iconic department store Illums Bolighus, which offers a wide range of designer furniture, lighting, and home accessories. Additionally, the streets of Strøget and Vesterbro are lined with trendy boutiques and independent shops, offering everything from vintage clothing to contemporary Danish fashion.

If you are looking for more affordable options, be sure to check out the many flea markets and secondhand stores located throughout the city. The popular outdoor market, Loppemarkedet, is a great place to find unique vintage clothing and homeware at bargain prices.

Stockholm, Sweden

Stockholm is a hub of Scandinavian fashion, design, and culture, making it an ideal destination for shoppers. The city is home to many well-known Swedish fashion brands, including Acne Studios, Filippa K, and H&M.

For luxury shopping, be sure to check out the exclusive department store Nordiska Kompaniet, which features a wide range of high-end fashion and homeware. Additionally, the trendy neighborhood of Södermalm is home to many independent boutiques and artisanal shops, offering everything from handmade jewelry to locally sourced food products.

If you are looking for more affordable shopping options, be sure to check out the many flea markets and vintage stores located throughout the city. The popular Hornstull Market and Old Touch Vintage Market are great places to find unique and affordable fashion and homeware.

Oslo, Norway

Oslo is known for its innovative and eco-friendly design, and it is a great place to shop for sustainable and locally made products. The city is home to many well-known Norwegian fashion brands, including Moods of Norway, Cathrine Hammel, and Oleana.

For sustainable fashion, be sure to check out the trendy boutique Fretex Unika, which offers a wide range of upcycled and secondhand clothing. Additionally, the popular Mathallen food hall is a great place to find artisanal food products and locally sourced ingredients.

If you are looking for more traditional Norwegian souvenirs, be sure to check out the many handicraft and souvenir shops located throughout the city. These shops offer a wide range of handcrafted products, including wool sweaters, wooden toys, and silver jewelry.

Helsinki, Finland

Helsinki is a city that is rich in design and culture, and it is a great place to shop for unique and innovative products. The city is home to many well-known Finnish fashion brands, including Marimekko, Ivana Helsinki, and Samuji.

For design lovers, be sure to check out the Design District, a neighborhood that is home to many independent boutiques and design studios. Additionally, the popular Market Square is a great place to find local food products and handicrafts.

If you are looking for more affordable shopping options, be sure to check out the many flea markets and secondhand stores located throughout the city. The popular Hietalahti Market Hall is a great place to find vintage clothing and homeware at bargain prices.

Tips for Shopping in Scandinavia on a Budget

While shopping in Scandinavia can be a great experience, it can also be quite expensive. To keep your expenses in check, here are some tips to help you shop in Scandinavia on a budget:

Shop at secondhand stores and flea markets: Scandinavia is home to many high-quality secondhand stores and flea markets where you can find unique and affordable items. Many of these shops offer designer clothing and homeware at a fraction of the cost of buying new.

- **Look for sales and discounts:** Many stores in Scandinavia offer discounts and sales throughout the year, especially during the end of season sales. Be sure to check the store's website or ask the sales staff about any current promotions.

- **Buy local products:** Locally made products are often less expensive than imported products, and they offer a unique and authentic Scandinavian experience. Look for locally made clothing, homeware, and food products to save money and support the local economy.

- **Use public transportation:** Taxis and private transportation can be expensive in Scandinavia, so consider using public transportation to get around. Many cities offer affordable day passes or tourist cards that include unlimited public transportation and discounts on attractions and shops.

- **Eat like a local:** Eating out can be expensive in Scandinavia, so consider eating like a local and visiting local food markets or grocery stores. You can find affordable and delicious local foods to try and save money on dining out.

CHAPTER 3

SCANDINAVIA TRAVEL ITINERARY

3 Days Scandinavia Itinerary

Day 1: Copenhagen, Denmark

Copenhagen is the capital city of Denmark and is known for its picturesque canals, colorful buildings, and trendy neighborhoods. Here is an itinerary for exploring Copenhagen in one day:

- **Morning:** Start your day with a visit to Nyhavn, a picturesque waterfront area that is lined with colorful buildings and cafes. You can take a boat tour of the canals or simply stroll around and take in the sights.

- **Midday:** Next, head to the iconic Tivoli Gardens, which is a popular amusement park and a national treasure of Denmark. Here, you can enjoy thrilling rides, beautiful gardens, and live entertainment.

- **Afternoon:** For lunch, head to Torvehallerne, a trendy food market that offers a wide range of local and international cuisine. Try some traditional Danish smørrebrød, open-faced sandwiches with various toppings.

- **Evening:** In the evening, head to the trendy neighborhood of Vesterbro, which is known for its hip bars, cafes, and shops.

Here, you can enjoy some of Copenhagen's famous craft beers or visit some of the independent shops and boutiques.

Estimated expenses for Day 1:

- Boat tour of Nyhavn: 80 DKK (11 USD)
- Tivoli Gardens admission: 130 DKK (19 USD)
- Lunch at Torvehallerne: 100 DKK (14 USD)
- Drinks and snacks in Vesterbro: 150 DKK (22 USD)

Total expenses: 460 DKK (66 USD)

Day 2: Stockholm, Sweden

Stockholm is the capital city of Sweden and is known for its stunning architecture, vibrant cultural scene, and beautiful parks. Here is an itinerary for exploring Stockholm in one day:

- **Morning:** Start your day by visiting Gamla Stan, the old town of Stockholm that is known for its charming cobblestone streets, colorful buildings, and historic landmarks. Here, you can visit the Royal Palace and the Nobel Museum.

- **Midday:** For lunch, head to Östermalm Saluhall, a popular food hall that offers a wide range of local and international cuisine. Try some traditional Swedish meatballs or seafood.

- **Afternoon:** Next, head to the trendy neighborhood of Södermalm, which is known for its independent boutiques, vintage shops, and art galleries. Here, you can shop for unique Scandinavian fashion and design products.

- **Evening:** In the evening, head to the popular nightlife area of Stureplan, which is home to many bars, clubs, and restaurants. Here, you can enjoy some of Stockholm's famous cocktails or dance the night away.

Estimated expenses for Day 2:

- Royal Palace and Nobel Museum admission: 230 SEK (26 USD)
- Lunch at Östermalm Saluhall: 150 SEK (17 USD)
- Shopping in Södermalm: 500 SEK (57 USD)
- Drinks and snacks in Stureplan: 300 SEK (34 USD)

Total expenses: 1180 SEK (134 USD)

Day 3: Oslo, Norway

Oslo is the capital city of Norway and is known for its stunning fjords, beautiful parks, and innovative design. Here is an itinerary for exploring Oslo in one day:

- **Morning:** Start your day by visiting Vigeland Park, a beautiful park that is home to over 200 bronze and granite sculptures by Gustav Vigeland. It is a must-visit attraction in Oslo and is free to enter.

- **Midday:** Next, head to the Oslo Opera House, which is known for its stunning modern design and beautiful waterfront location. You can take a d tour of the building or simply enjoy the views from the rooftop.

- **Afternoon:** For lunch, head to Mathallen Oslo, a popular food hall that offers a wide range of local and international cuisine. Try some traditional Norwegian seafood or cheese.

- **Evening:** In the evening, head to the trendy neighborhood of Grünerløkka, which is known for its independent shops, cafes, and bars. Here, you can enjoy some of Oslo's famous craft beers or visit some of the local art galleries.

Estimated expenses for Day 3:

- Vigeland Park admission: Free
- Oslo Opera House d tour: 150 NOK (17 USD)
- Lunch at Mathallen Oslo: 200 NOK (23 USD)
- Shopping in Grünerløkka: 500 NOK (57 USD)
- Drinks and snacks in Grünerløkka: 300 NOK (34 USD)

Total expenses: 1150 NOK (131 USD)

Total estimated expenses for the 3-day itinerary: 2790 DKK/381 USD/324 EUR/282 GBP

Note: The estimated expenses are based on the assumption of an average traveler's spending habits and do not include accommodation or transportation costs, which can vary depending on the mode of transportation and type of accommodation chosen.

7 Days Scandinavia Itinerary

Day 1: Copenhagen

- **Morning:** Start your day with a visit to the iconic Little Mermaid statue, located in the harbor of Copenhagen. Then, head to Nyhavn, a picturesque waterfront area filled with colorful buildings, restaurants, and cafes. Take a boat tour of the canals to see the city from a different perspective.

- **Afternoon:** For lunch, try some traditional Danish open-faced sandwiches, known as smørrebrød. Then, visit Tivoli Gardens, the world's second-oldest amusement park. It's a great place to relax and enjoy the beautiful gardens, live entertainment, and rides.

- **Evening:** In the evening, head to the trendy neighborhood of Vesterbro, where you can enjoy a variety of bars, cafes, and restaurants. Try some Danish craft beer or visit some of the local art galleries.

Estimated expenses for Day 1:

- Little Mermaid statue: Free

- Boat tour of the canals: 90 DKK (14 USD)

- Lunch of smørrebrød: 100 DKK (16 USD)

- Tivoli Gardens admission: 140 DKK (22 USD)

- Dinner and drinks in Vesterbro: 300 DKK (47 USD)

Total expenses: 630 DKK (99 USD)

Day 2: Copenhagen

- **Morning:** Start your day by visiting Christiansborg Palace, the seat of the Danish Parliament. Take a d tour to learn about the country's history and politics. Then, head to the National Museum of Denmark, which offers a fascinating collection of artifacts from prehistoric times to the present day.

- **Afternoon:** For lunch, try some traditional Danish hot dogs from one of the city's many street vendors. Then, visit the Carlsberg Brewery, where you can learn about the history of the famous beer and enjoy a tasting.

- **Evening:** In the evening, head to the trendy neighborhood of Nørrebro, which is known for its multicultural vibe and independent shops. Here, you can enjoy some live music, cocktails, or try some local street food.

Estimated expenses for Day 2:

- Christiansborg Palace d tour: 100 DKK (16 USD)
- National Museum of Denmark admission: Free
- Lunch of hot dogs: 50 DKK (8 USD)
- Carlsberg Brewery admission and tasting: 95 DKK (15 USD)
- Dinner and drinks in Nørrebro: 300 DKK (47 USD)

Total expenses: 545 DKK (86 USD)

Day 3: Stockholm

- **Morning:** Take a flight from Copenhagen to Stockholm, which takes about an hour. Once you arrive, start your day with a visit to the Vasa Museum, which houses the world's only preserved 17th-century warship. It's a fascinating piece of history and a must-visit attraction in Stockholm.
- **Afternoon:** For lunch, try some traditional Swedish meatballs or herring. Then, visit the Royal Palace, which is one of the largest palaces in Europe and home to the Swedish royal family. Take a d tour to see the impressive state rooms and learn about the country's monarchy.
- **Evening:** In the evening, head to the trendy neighborhood of Södermalm, which is known for its vintage shops, cafes, and bars. Here, you can enjoy some Swedish craft beer or visit some of the local art galleries.

Estimated expenses for Day 3:

- Flight from Copenhagen to Stockholm: 500 SEK (56 USD)
- Vasa Museum admission
- Vasa Museum admission: 150 SEK (17 USD)
- Lunch of Swedish meatballs or herring: 100 SEK (11 USD)
- Royal Palace d tour: 160 SEK (18 USD)
- Dinner and drinks in Södermalm: 300 SEK (34 USD)

Total expenses: 1,210 SEK (136 USD)

Day 4: Stockholm

- **Morning:** Start your day with a visit to the historic Old Town, also known as Gamla Stan. It's a charming area with narrow streets, colorful buildings, and medieval architecture. Visit the Royal Armoury, which showcases a collection of armor and weapons used by Swedish kings and queens.
- **Afternoon:** For lunch, try some traditional Swedish pea soup or toast skagen, which is a popular seafood dish. Then, visit the ABBA Museum, which celebrates the famous Swedish pop group. It's a fun interactive museum that's great for all ages.
- **Evening:** In the evening, head to the trendy neighborhood of Östermalm, which is known for its high-end boutiques,

restaurants, and bars. Here, you can enjoy some cocktails, live music, or try some local delicacies.

Estimated expenses for Day 4:

- Old Town walking tour: 200 SEK (22 USD)
- Royal Armoury admission: 160 SEK (18 USD)
- Lunch of pea soup or toast skagen: 100 SEK (11 USD)
- ABBA Museum admission: 250 SEK (28 USD)
- Dinner and drinks in Östermalm: 400 SEK (45 USD)

Total expenses: 1,110 SEK (125 USD)

Day 5: Oslo

- **Morning:** Take a train from Stockholm to Oslo, which takes about 5 hours. Once you arrive, start your day with a visit to the famous Vigeland Park, which features over 200 bronze, granite, and cast iron sculptures by Gustav Vigeland.
- **Afternoon:** For lunch, try some traditional Norwegian salmon or cod. Then, visit the Munch Museum, which houses the largest collection of paintings and drawings by the famous Norwegian artist, Edvard Munch.
- **Evening:** In the evening, head to the trendy neighborhood of Grünerløkka, which is known for its street art, independent

shops, and nightlife. Here, you can enjoy some craft beer, live music, or try some local street food.

Estimated expenses for Day 5:

- Train from Stockholm to Oslo: 600 NOK (70 USD)
- Vigeland Park admission: Free
- Lunch of Norwegian salmon or cod: 150 NOK (18 USD)
- Munch Museum admission: 120 NOK (14 USD)
- Dinner and drinks in Grünerløkka: 400 NOK (47 USD)

Total expenses: 1,270 NOK (149 USD)

Day 6: Oslo

1. **Morning:** Start your day with a visit to the famous Viking Ship Museum, which showcases three Viking ships that were excavated from burial mounds in the Oslo fjord.
2. **Afternoon:** For lunch, try some traditional Norwegian waffles or rømmegrøt, which is a sour cream porridge. Then, visit the Oslo Opera House, which is a modern and impressive building located **on the waterfront.**
3. **Evening:** In the evening, head to the trendy neighborhood of Aker Brygge, which is known for its upscale restaurants, bars, and shops. Here, you can enjoy some cocktails, live music, or try some local seafood.

Estimated expenses for Day 6:

- Viking Ship Museum admission: 120 NOK (14 USD)
- Lunch of Norwegian waffles or rømmegrøt: 100 N
- Oslo Opera House d tour: 150 NOK (18 USD)
- Dinner and drinks in Aker Brygge: 500 NOK (59 USD)

Total expenses: 870 NOK (103 USD)

Day 7: Copenhagen

- **Morning:** Take a flight from Oslo to Copenhagen, which takes about 1 hour. Once you arrive, start your day with a visit to the famous Nyhavn harbor, which is lined with colorful buildings, restaurants, and cafes.
- **Afternoon:** For lunch, try some traditional Danish smørrebrød, which is an open-faced sandwich with various toppings. Then, visit the famous Tivoli Gardens, which is a historic amusement park with rides, games, and gardens.
- **Evening:** In the evening, head to the trendy neighborhood of Nørrebro, which is known for its street art, independent shops, and nightlife. Here, you can enjoy some craft beer, live music, or try some local street food.

Estimated expenses for Day 7:

- Flight from Oslo to Copenhagen: 600 DKK (95 USD)

- Nyhavn visit: Free

- Lunch of Danish smørrebrød: 100 DKK (16 USD)

- Tivoli Gardens admission: 140 DKK (22 USD)

- Dinner and drinks in Nørrebro: 400 DKK (64 USD)

Total expenses: 1,240 DKK (197 USD)

Overall estimated expenses for the 7-day itinerary:

- Transportation: 3,630 SEK (408 USD)

- Accommodation: 5,250 SEK (590 USD)

- Food and drinks: 4,200 SEK (472 USD)

- Attractions and activities: 2,710 SEK (304 USD)

- Total expenses: 15,790 SEK (1,774 USD)

Note: These expenses are just estimates and can vary depending on the season, exchange rates, and personal preferences. It's always a good idea to research and plan ahead to get the best deals and prices. Additionally, there are many free or low-cost activities and attractions in Scandinavia, so be sure to take advantage of those as well.

CHAPTER 4

PLANING A TRIP TO SCANDINAVIA

What to Pack For Your Trip

Warm clothing

Scandinavia is known for its chilly weather, especially during the winter months. Therefore, packing warm clothing is essential. Start with a few pairs of thermal leggings and tops, a warm jacket or coat, and some gloves and hats. Don't forget to pack a scarf, as it can help you keep your neck warm and prevent colds. Pack some woolen socks and comfortable boots or sneakers to keep your feet warm.

● **Waterproof clothing**

The weather in Scandinavia can be unpredictable, so it's essential to pack waterproof clothing. Invest in a high-quality raincoat or waterproof jacket that can keep you dry during unexpected rain showers. Make sure you pack a pair of waterproof pants or leggings, especially if you plan to do some outdoor activities like hiking or trekking. A waterproof backpack can also come in handy to keep your belongings safe and dry.

● **Camera gear**

Scandinavia is a photographer's paradise, with breathtaking landscapes, colorful buildings, and beautiful architecture.

Therefore, it's essential to pack a good camera and some extra batteries. A tripod can also be useful to take stable shots, especially in low light conditions. Don't forget to pack an extra memory card to store all your photographs.

- **Power adapter**

Scandinavia uses different types of power outlets than other parts of the world, so it's essential to pack a power adapter to charge your electronic devices. You can either buy a universal adapter that works with different types of outlets or buy a specific adapter for Scandinavia.

- **Cash and credit cards**

While most places in Scandinavia accept credit cards, it's always a good idea to carry some cash with you, especially if you plan to visit smaller towns or villages. You can exchange currency at banks or currency exchange offices, but it's better to check the exchange rates beforehand to avoid overpaying.

- **Medications**

If you take any medications regularly, make sure you pack them in your carry-on luggage. It's also a good idea to carry a small first aid kit with you, including items like pain relievers, band-aids, and antiseptic wipes.

- **Travel documents**

Don't forget to pack all your travel documents, including your passport, visa (if required), and travel insurance. Make sure you keep them in a safe place, like a passport holder or a money belt. It's also a good idea to keep electronic copies of your travel documents, like a scanned copy of your passport, in case you lose the original.

- **Maps and books**

While most places in Scandinavia have good internet connectivity, it's always a good idea to carry physical maps and books with you. You can buy books online or at a local bookstore. Maps can be downloaded from the internet or purchased at local bookstores.

- **Toiletries**

Pack all your toiletries, including toothbrush, toothpaste, shampoo, conditioner, soap, and deodorant. If you have any specific toiletries that you prefer to use, like a particular brand of face wash, make sure you pack them as well. It's also a good idea to pack a small travel-size bottle of hand sanitizer.

- **Outdoor gear**

If you plan to do some outdoor activities like hiking, skiing, or snowboarding, make sure you pack appropriate outdoor gear. Pack a good pair of hiking boots or sturdy sneakers, warm socks, and comfortable clothes that are suitable for outdoor activities. If you plan to ski or snowboard, make sure you pack a good quality ski jacket, snow pants, gloves, and goggles.

- **Swimsuit**

Scandinavia has several natural hot springs and swimming pools, especially in Iceland, where swimming is a popular activity. Therefore, it's a good idea to pack a swimsuit, even if you're visiting during the winter months. You can enjoy a relaxing soak in one of the many hot springs or even try ice swimming, a popular activity in Scandinavia.

- **Casual clothing**

While Scandinavia is known for its trendy and stylish fashion, it's also a place where casual clothing is acceptable. Pack comfortable clothes like jeans, t-shirts, and sweaters that you can wear during the day or for a night out. Scandinavia is known for its hygge culture, where comfort and coziness are highly valued, so don't hesitate to pack some comfortable loungewear for relaxing evenings.

- **Travel-sized laundry detergent**

If you plan to travel for an extended period, it's a good idea to pack travel-sized laundry detergent. You can wash your clothes in the sink or bathtub and hang them to dry overnight. This can save you money on laundry expenses and help you travel light.

- **Portable charger**

Scandinavia has several beautiful natural landscapes and outdoor activities, which can drain your phone battery quickly. Pack a portable charger to keep your electronic devices charged throughout the day.

- **Snacks**

While Scandinavia has some of the best food in the world, it's always a good idea to pack some snacks for long bus or train rides. You can pack some energy bars, nuts, or dried fruits that can help you keep your energy levels up during long journeys.

Scandinavia With Children

- **Visit amusement parks**

There are several theme parks in Scandinavia that are ideal for families with children. Tivoli Gardens in Copenhagen, Denmark, is one of the world's oldest amusement parks, offering rides, games, and live performances. Another popular theme park in Gothenburg, Sweden, is Liseberg, which has roller coasters, carousels, and a water park.

- **Investigate the outdoors**

Scandinavia is well-known for its stunning natural scenery and outdoor activities. In the region's national parks and forests, families with children can go hiking, biking, fishing, and camping. During the winter, families can go skiing, snowboarding, or sledding in Scandinavia's many ski resorts.

- **Discover Viking history.**

Scandinavia has a rich Viking history, which families with children can learn about by visiting museums and historical sites. In Oslo, Norway, the Viking Ship Museum displays well-preserved Viking ships, artifacts, and interactive exhibits. The Viking Village in Denmark gives families a taste of Viking life through workshops, games, and demonstrations.

- **Go to zoos and aquariums.**

Scandinavia is home to a number of zoos and aquariums that are ideal for families with children. In Stockholm, Sweden, the Skansen Open-Air Museum has a zoo with Nordic animals such as reindeer, moose, and wolves. The Bergen Aquarium in Norway houses a diverse array of fish, penguins, and seals.

- **Discover Scandinavian culture.**

Families with children can experience Scandinavian culture through food, music, and festivals. Traditional Scandinavian dishes such as meatballs, salmon, and rye bread are available for families. Scandinavian music is popular as well, and families can attend concerts or music festivals such as the Roskilde Festival in Denmark or Way Out West in Sweden.

Planning a Family-Friendly Scandinavian Vacation

- **Choose family-friendly lodging.**

When traveling to Scandinavia with children, it is critical to select family-friendly accommodations. Look for hotels or apartments with amenities such as a kids' play area, a pool, or a kitchenette. Airbnb is also an excellent choice for families, as you can rent a house or apartment large enough to accommodate the entire family.

- **Pack weather-appropriate clothing.**

Because the weather in Scandinavia is unpredictable, it is critical to pack appropriately. Summer temperatures can range from mild to warm, so pack light clothing such as t-shirts, shorts, and sandals. Temperatures can be very cold during the winter months, so bring warm clothing such as winter jackets, boots, and gloves.

- **Make plans for outdoor activities.**

Scandinavia is known for its beautiful natural landscapes, so planning outdoor activities with children is a great idea. Hiking, biking, and fishing are excellent summer activities, while skiing, snowboarding, and sledding are excellent winter activities. Pack appropriate outdoor gear and plan activities that are appropriate for children.

- **Make use of public transportation.**

Trains, buses, and ferries are among the many modes of public transportation available in Scandinavia. Taking public transportation is an excellent way to save money while traveling with children. Many Scandinavian cities also have bike rental programs, which are a great way for families to explore the city.

Look for family-friendly attractions.

- **Before you take your children to Scandinavia,**

Research family-friendly attractions in Scandinavia before your trip. There are many attractions and activities suitable for children, but planning ahead is essential to ensure that you have enough time to see everything you want to see. Consider purchasing your tickets in advance to avoid long lines.

● **Bring snacks and beverages.**

When traveling with children, it is critical to bring snacks and drinks. Bring fruit, nuts, and granola bars, as well as water bottles or juice boxes. This will save you money on costly snacks and drinks while also providing your children with something to eat and drink throughout the day.

● **Be adaptable in your travel plans.**

Traveling with children can be unpredictable, so make sure your itinerary is adaptable. Allow plenty of time for rest and relaxation and be prepared to change your plans if necessary. It is preferable to take your time and enjoy the trip rather than cramming too many activities into one day.

● **Consider a family tour or a tour .**

Consider booking a family tour or if you're unsure how to plan a family-friendly trip to Scandinavia. There are numerous companies that specialize in family travel and can assist you in planning a trip that is appropriate for your family's needs. A tour or can also teach you about the region's history, culture, and attractions.

● **Bring children's entertainment.**

Long flights or car rides can be exhausting for children, so bring something to keep them entertained. Bring books, coloring books, puzzles, or handheld games to keep kids entertained on the trip.

- **Be mindful of local customs.**

Scandinavia has a distinct culture, and it is critical to respect local customs when traveling with children. Before you travel, learn about local customs such as how to greet people, what to wear, and how to behave in public places. Respecting local customs will make your trip more enjoyable for you and your children.

Night Life In Scandinavia

Copenhagen, the capital of Denmark, is home to some of the most exciting nightlife in the region. The city's famous street, Strøget, offers a plethora of bars, pubs, and nightclubs, making it the perfect destination for those who want to experience a night out. Many of the bars in Copenhagen are located in old buildings, giving them a unique character and charm. The city is also famous for its craft beer scene, with many breweries offering tours and tastings.

One of the most popular nightclubs in Copenhagen is Culture Box, which offers a unique blend of techno, house, and electronic music. The club has a reputation for hosting some of the best DJs from around the world, making it a must-visit destination for music lovers. Another popular club is Rust, which offers live music performances and a laid-back atmosphere. If you're looking for a more upscale experience, head to the exclusive nightclub, Lusso, where you can dance the night away while sipping on champagne.

Stockholm, the capital of Sweden, is also known for its exciting nightlife scene. The city's Old Town is home to many cozy pubs and bars, offering a relaxed atmosphere for those who prefer a quieter night out. For a more lively experience, head to the Södermalm district, which is known for its trendy bars and nightclubs. The district is particularly popular with the younger crowd, with many venues offering a mix of indie and electronic music.

One of the most popular nightclubs in Stockholm is Berns, which is located in a beautiful 19th-century building. The club has a reputation for hosting some of the biggest names in music, and its main hall is considered one of the most beautiful in the city. Another popular venue is Debaser Medis, which offers live music performances and a relaxed atmosphere. The club is known for hosting some of the best indie and alternative bands from around the world.

Oslo, the capital of Norway, may be known for its stunning fjords and mountains, but it also offers a bustling nightlife scene. The city's Grünerløkka district is home to many trendy bars and clubs, with a mix of electronic and indie music. The district is particularly popular with the younger crowd, with many venues offering a laid-back atmosphere and affordable drinks.

One of the most popular nightclubs in Oslo is The Villa, which is known for its unique design and high-quality music. The club offers a mix of techno, house, and electronic music, and its rooftop terrace offers stunning views of the city. Another popular venue is Blå, which offers live music performances and a cozy atmosphere. The club is known for hosting some of the best jazz, blues, and indie acts in the city.

Helsinki, the capital of Finland, may be one of the smallest cities in the region, but it still offers a vibrant nightlife scene. The city's Kallio district is home to many bars and nightclubs, with a mix of electronic and indie music. The district is particularly popular with the younger crowd, with many venues offering affordable drinks and a relaxed atmosphere.

One of the most popular nightclubs in Helsinki is Kaiku, which is known for its unique design and high-quality music. The club offers a mix of techno, house, and electronic music, and its sound system is considered one of the best in the city. Another popular venue is Ääniö, which offers live music performances and a laid-back atmosphere. The club is known for hosting some of the best indie and alternative acts from around the world.

One of the unique features of Helsinki's nightlife is the sauna culture. Saunas are an essential part of Finnish culture, and many nightclubs and bars have saunas on their premises. For example, Löyly is a popular sauna and restaurant in Helsinki, offering a unique experience for those who want to relax and unwind after a night out.

One thing that sets Scandinavia's nightlife scene apart from others around the world is the focus on sustainability and environmentalism. Many clubs and bars in the region prioritize sustainable practices, such as using renewable energy sources and reducing waste. For example, The Villa in Oslo has implemented a green roof, which helps to reduce energy consumption and greenhouse gas emissions.

In addition to traditional bars and nightclubs, Scandinavia also offers a unique nightlife experience with its cultural events and festivals. For example, the Stockholm Culture Festival is a five-day event that takes place every year in August, offering a mix of music, dance, theater, and art. The event attracts visitors from around the world and is a great way to experience the city's cultural scene.

Another popular festival is the Roskilde Festival, which takes place every year in Denmark. The festival is one of the largest music events in Europe, attracting over 130,000 visitors each year. The festival offers a mix of music genres, from rock and pop to electronic and hip-hop, making it a must-visit destination for music lovers.

People and Culture

The People of Scandinavia

The people of Scandinavia are known for their strong work ethic, honesty, and social responsibility. They are generally reserved and introverted, but once you get to know them, they are warm and welcoming. The Scandinavian countries are some of the most egalitarian in the world, with a strong commitment to social welfare and gender equality.

The Scandinavian countries are also known for their high levels of education and literacy. The region has some of the best education systems in the world, and it is not uncommon for people to have multiple degrees. This focus on education has led to a highly skilled workforce, which has been instrumental in the region's economic success.

Culture and Traditions

Scandinavian culture is characterized by its simplicity, minimalism, and functionalism. The region is known for its clean and simple design, which is evident in everything from furniture to architecture. Scandinavian design is often described as "form follows function," with a focus on practicality and usability.

Another important aspect of Scandinavian culture is its connection to nature. The region's stunning natural landscapes, including fjords, mountains, and forests, have inspired many of the region's traditions and cultural practices. For example, in Norway, there is a long tradition of hiking in the mountains, which is known as "friluftsliv" or "open-air living." This tradition emphasizes the importance of being in nature and connecting with the environment.

In addition to its connection to nature, Scandinavian culture is also characterized by its strong sense of community. This is evident in the region's many festivals and celebrations, which bring people together to celebrate their shared history and traditions. For example, in Sweden, there is a tradition of celebrating Midsummer, which is the longest day of the year. This festival involves dancing around a maypole, eating traditional foods, and drinking schnapps.

Food and Drink

Scandinavian cuisine is known for its simplicity and focus on fresh, locally sourced ingredients. The region's long coastline provides a rich source of seafood, including salmon, herring, and cod. These ingredients are often prepared in simple ways, such as smoked or pickled, to bring out their natural flavors.

Another important aspect of Scandinavian cuisine is its connection to nature. Many traditional dishes are based on foraged ingredients, such as mushrooms, berries, and herbs. For example, in Sweden, there is a tradition of "fika," which involves taking a break in the afternoon to have coffee and pastries. These pastries often include ingredients such as lingonberries and cardamom, which are commonly found in the Swedish countryside.

When it comes to alcohol, Scandinavia is known for its love of beer and aquavit. Beer is the most popular alcoholic drink in the region, with a long tradition of brewing. In Norway, there is a tradition of "juleøl," or Christmas beer, which is a dark, spiced beer that is only available during the holiday season. Aquavit is a distilled spirit that is flavored with herbs and spices such as caraway and dill. It is often consumed with traditional Scandinavian dishes, such as pickled herring.

Art and Literature

Scandinavia has a rich tradition of art and literature, which is often inspired by the region's natural landscapes and culture. The region is known for its minimalist design and functionalism, which is evident in its art and architecture.

One of the most famous Scandinavian artists is the Norwegian painter Edvard Munch, who is known for his iconic painting "The Scream." Munch's work is characterized by its intense emotion and expressionism, which was a departure from the traditional academic style of painting that was popular at the time.

Scandinavian literature is also rich and diverse, with a long tradition of storytelling and poetry. One of the most famous Scandinavian writers is the Danish author Hans Christian Andersen, who is known for his fairy tales such as "The Little Mermaid" and "The Ugly Duckling." Another famous writer is the Swedish author Astrid Lindgren, who is known for her children's books such as "Pippi Longstocking."

Music and Film

Scandinavian music has a long and rich history, with a variety of genres including folk, pop, and heavy metal. One of the most famous Scandinavian musicians is the Norwegian composer Edvard Grieg, who is known for his classical compositions such as "Peer Gynt."

In recent years, Scandinavia has also produced a number of successful pop and electronic music artists, such as ABBA, Roxette, and Avicii. The region is also known for its heavy metal music, with bands such as Metallica and Iron Maiden citing Scandinavian bands like Bathory and Mercyful Fate as influences.

Scandinavian cinema is also highly regarded, with a long tradition of producing critically acclaimed films. The region has produced a number of famous directors, including the Danish director Lars von Trier, who is known for his controversial and provocative films such as "Breaking the Waves" and "Antichrist." Other notable Scandinavian filmmakers include the Swedish director Ingmar Bergman and the Danish director Susanne Bier.

Tipping in Scandinavia

Tipping is a common practice in many countries around the world, where customers leave a small amount of money as a gratuity for their service. However, in Scandinavia, the practice of tipping is not as widespread as it is in other parts of the world. This is due to several cultural and social factors that have shaped the attitudes towards tipping in the region.

Cultural Differences

One of the main reasons why tipping is not as common in Scandinavia is because of the cultural differences in the region. The Nordic countries, which include Denmark, Finland, Norway, Sweden, and Iceland, have a strong welfare state and a high standard of living. This means that employees in service industries, such as restaurants and cafes, are generally well paid and do not rely on tips as a significant part of their income.

In addition, there is a strong sense of egalitarianism in Scandinavian culture, where everyone is expected to be treated equally regardless of their social status or wealth. This means that tipping can be seen as a way of creating a social hierarchy, where those who can afford to leave larger tips are given preferential treatment over those who cannot.

Service Standards

Another factor that contributes to the low tipping culture in Scandinavia is the high level of service standards in the region. In general, service in Scandinavia is known for being efficient, friendly, and professional. This means that customers are less likely to feel the need to leave a tip as a way of incentivizing good service.

In fact, some argue that tipping can actually have a negative effect on service standards, as it can create a culture of entitlement where employees feel that they are entitled to receive a tip regardless of the quality of their service.

Cultural Etiquette

Despite the low tipping culture in Scandinavia, there are still some situations where tipping is expected or appreciated. For example, in upscale restaurants, it is customary to leave a small tip of around 5-10% of the total bill. This is seen as a way of showing appreciation for the high quality of service and the experience provided.

In addition, it is also common to round up the bill to the nearest whole number as a way of showing appreciation for the service provided. This is especially true in cafes and bars where customers may order drinks or small snacks.

However, it is important to note that in many cases, tipping is not expected and may even be seen as inappropriate. This is especially true in situations where the service is already included in the price, such as in taxis or at hotels.

CHAPTER 5

DENMARK, NORWAY, ICELAND, FINLAND & SWEDEN

Top 5 Events In Denmark To Attend

Roskilde Festival

Roskilde Festival is one of the most renowned music festivals in Europe, and it takes place in Roskilde, Denmark. It is an annual event that is held during the summer, typically in late June or early July. The festival features a diverse range of music genres, including rock, pop, hip hop, electronic, and world music. In addition to music, the festival offers a range of cultural activities and experiences that make it a must-attend event.

One of the highlights of Roskilde Festival is its impressive lineup of musical acts. The festival typically features over 175 artists from around the world, with a mix of well-known and up-and-coming artists. Some of the most notable performers in recent years have included The Rolling Stones, Paul McCartney, Beyoncé, Kendrick Lamar, and Arctic Monkeys.

Beyond the music, Roskilde Festival offers a range of cultural experiences that make it a unique event. The festival has a strong focus on sustainability, with a range of initiatives aimed at reducing its environmental impact. There are also several art installations and workshops that offer visitors the chance to engage with art and culture in a hands-on way.

In terms of when to attend, the best time to visit Roskilde Festival is during the summer months. The festival typically takes place over four days, from Thursday to Sunday, in late June or early July. The weather during this time is generally warm and sunny, making it the perfect time to enjoy outdoor music and cultural activities.

Aarhus Festiva

Aarhus Festuge (Aarhus Festival Week) is a cultural event held annually in Aarhus, Denmark. It is one of the largest cultural festivals in Scandinavia and attracts visitors from all over the world. The festival takes place over 10 days in late August or early September and offers a diverse range of cultural experiences.

One of the highlights of Aarhus Festuge is its wide range of cultural events. The festival features performances by international musicians, artists, and actors, as well as local Danish acts. Visitors can enjoy music, theater, dance, and visual art performances, as well as literary events, films, and food experiences.

Another unique aspect of Aarhus Festuge is its focus on public art and installations. The festival brings together international and local artists to create large-scale art installations throughout the city, transforming public spaces into interactive and immersive environments. These installations often reflect the festival's theme for the year, which changes annually.

Visitors to Aarhus Festuge can also participate in a range of workshops, seminars, and d tours. These events offer the chance to learn more about the festival's theme and the cultural context of the performances and installations.

In terms of when to attend, the best time to experience Aarhus Festuge is during the summer months, typically in late August or early September. The weather during this time is generally mild and pleasant, making it easy to enjoy outdoor events and explore the city.

Copenhagen Jazz Festival

Copenhagen Jazz Festival is one of the largest jazz festivals in Europe, and it takes place in the Danish capital of Copenhagen every summer. The festival attracts thousands of jazz lovers from around the world, who come to enjoy an extensive and diverse program of jazz music.

One of the highlights of Copenhagen Jazz Festival is its impressive lineup of musicians. The festival typically features over 1200 concerts, with more than 130 venues spread throughout the city. The program features both well-known international artists and emerging local talents, making it an excellent opportunity to discover new music and support up-and-coming jazz musicians.

In addition to the music, Copenhagen Jazz Festival offers a range of cultural experiences. There are workshops, masterclasses, and talks that allow visitors to engage with jazz music in a more in-depth way. There are also several art exhibitions and installations that explore the intersection between jazz and other art forms.

The festival also has a strong focus on sustainability, with several initiatives aimed at reducing its environmental impact. Visitors can participate in bike tours and other green activities, making it a great way to explore Copenhagen while minimizing their carbon footprint.

In terms of when to attend, the best time to visit Copenhagen Jazz Festival is during the summer months, typically in late June or early July. The weather during this time is generally warm and pleasant, making it the perfect time to enjoy outdoor concerts and cultural activities.

Tivoli Gardens

Tivoli Gardens is a popular amusement park in Copenhagen, Denmark. It is one of the world's oldest amusement parks, having opened in 1843, and is a popular attraction for Copenhagen visitors. Tivoli Gardens has rides, games, and attractions, as well as cultural experiences and events.

Tivoli Gardens' impressive range of rides and attractions is one of its highlights. Roller coasters, water rides, and other thrill rides are available, as well as a variety of gentler rides suitable for younger children. Arcades, bumper cars, and carnival-style games are also available for visitors to enjoy.

Tivoli Gardens provides a variety of cultural experiences in addition to rides and attractions. Throughout the park, there are several theaters and stages that host a variety of live performances such as ballet, opera, and theater. There are also a number of art exhibitions and installations, as well as a variety of restaurants and cafes serving traditional Danish fare.

The winter holiday season is one of the best times to visit Tivoli Gardens. With thousands of lights, Christmas decorations, and seasonal activities, the park is transformed into a magical winter wonderland. Ice skating, Christmas markets, and live entertainment are available to visitors, making it an ideal place to get into the holiday spirit.

Danish Christmas Markets

Danish Christmas Markets are a beloved tradition in Denmark, offering visitors the opportunity to experience the festive holiday season in a unique and charming way. These markets are typically held throughout the country, with each market featuring its own unique atmosphere, food, and crafts.

One of the highlights of Danish Christmas Markets is the traditional Danish cuisine that is served. Visitors can sample classic Danish dishes such as æbleskiver (round, fluffy pancakes), gløgg (mulled wine), and Christmas cookies. There are also stalls selling traditional crafts, such as handmade ornaments, pottery, and textiles, making it a great opportunity to pick up unique gifts and souvenirs.

In addition to the food and crafts, Danish Christmas Markets also offer a range of activities and entertainment. There are often live music performances, carol singing, and even visits from Santa Claus himself. Children can enjoy carnival rides and games, while adults can browse the stalls and enjoy the festive atmosphere.

The best time to visit Danish Christmas Markets is typically in the weeks leading up to Christmas, from late November to mid-December. During this time, the markets are at their most festive, with Christmas lights and decorations creating a magical atmosphere. Copenhagen is home to several of the most popular markets, including the Tivoli Christmas Market and the Christmas Market at Nyhavn.

Top 5 Must-Try Best Local Cuisine in Denmark

1. Smørrebrød

Smørrebrød is a traditional open-faced sandwich that is popular in Denmark. It consists of a slice of rye bread (rugbrød) topped with various toppings such as meat, fish, cheese, and vegetables. Smørrebrød is a staple food in Denmark and is enjoyed as a snack, lunch, or even as a light dinner.

To get Smørrebrød in Denmark, there are several options available. One way is to visit a traditional Danish restaurant that specializes in Smørrebrød. These restaurants offer a wide variety of toppings and are a great way to experience the authentic flavors of Denmark.

Another way to get Smørrebrød is to visit a local bakery or supermarket. Many bakeries and supermarkets in Denmark offer Smørrebrød to-go, which is a convenient option for those who want to enjoy this traditional Danish food on-the-go.

The cost of Smørrebrød in Denmark can vary depending on where you purchase it. At a traditional Danish restaurant, the cost of Smørrebrød can range from 70-150 DKK (approximately 11-23 USD) per sandwich. At a bakery or supermarket, the cost of Smørrebrød is usually lower and can range from 20-50 DKK (approximately 3-8 USD) per sandwich.

2. Frikadeller

Frikadeller is a traditional Danish dish that is similar to meatballs. It is typically made with a mixture of ground pork and beef, and is seasoned with onions, salt, and pepper. Frikadeller is a popular food in Denmark, and it is often served with potatoes and gravy.

To get Frikadeller in Denmark, there are several options available. One way is to visit a traditional Danish restaurant that specializes in Danish cuisine. These restaurants often have Frikadeller on their menu, along with other classic Danish dishes.

Another way to get Frikadeller is to visit a local bakery or supermarket. Many bakeries and supermarkets in Denmark offer pre-made Frikadeller that can be taken home and reheated for a quick and easy meal.

The cost of Frikadeller in Denmark can vary depending on where you purchase it. At a traditional Danish restaurant, the cost of Frikadeller can range from 100-200 DKK (approximately 15-30 USD) for a plate with sides. At a bakery or supermarket, the cost of Frikadeller is usually lower and can range from 20-50 DKK (approximately 3-8 USD) for a package of pre-made Frikadeller.

3. Flæskesteg

Flæskesteg is a traditional Danish dish that consists of roasted pork with crispy skin. It is a staple food in Denmark and is often served with potatoes, gravy, and red cabbage.

To get Flæskesteg in Denmark, there are several options available. One way is to visit a traditional Danish restaurant that specializes in Danish cuisine. These restaurants often have Flæskesteg on their menu, along with other classic Danish dishes.

Another way to get Flæskesteg is to visit a local butcher shop or supermarket. Many butcher shops and supermarkets in Denmark offer pre-seasoned Flæskesteg that can be taken home and roasted for a traditional Danish meal.

The cost of Flæskesteg in Denmark can vary depending on where you purchase it. At a traditional Danish restaurant, the cost of Flæskesteg can range from 150-250 DKK (approximately 23-38 USD) for a plate with sides. At a butcher shop or supermarket, the cost of Flæskesteg is usually lower and can range from 60-150 DKK (approximately 9-23 USD) for a piece of pork that can serve 2-4 people.

4. Rugbrød

Rugbrød is a traditional Danish rye bread that is a staple food in Denmark. It is a dark, dense bread that is made with a combination of rye flour, wheat flour, and sourdough starter. Rugbrød is known for its rich, nutty flavor and its ability to keep you feeling full and satisfied for hours.

To get Rugbrød in Denmark, there are several options available. One way is to visit a local bakery that specializes in Danish breads. These bakeries often offer a variety of Rugbrød, including different types of seeds and grains mixed in.

Another way to get Rugbrød is to visit a supermarket or grocery store. Most supermarkets in Denmark offer pre-packaged Rugbrød that can be taken home and enjoyed as part of a traditional Danish meal.

The cost of Rugbrød in Denmark can vary depending on where you purchase it. At a local bakery, the cost of Rugbrød can range from 20-30 DKK (approximately 3-5 USD) per loaf. At a supermarket or grocery store, the cost of Rugbrød is usually lower and can range from 10-20 DKK (approximately 2-3 USD) per loaf.

5. Æbleflæsk

Æbleflæsk is a traditional Danish dish that consists of fried pork belly and apples. It is a popular dish in Denmark, particularly during the fall and winter months when apples are in season.

To get Æbleflæsk in Denmark, there are several options available. One way is to visit a traditional Danish restaurant that specializes in Danish cuisine. These restaurants often have Æbleflæsk on their menu, along with other classic Danish dishes.

Another way to get Æbleflæsk is to make it at home. The ingredients for Æbleflæsk, including pork belly, apples, and onions, can be found at most supermarkets and grocery stores in Denmark.

The cost of Æbleflæsk in Denmark can vary depending on where you purchase it. At a traditional Danish restaurant, the cost of Æbleflæsk can range from 100-200 DKK (approximately 15-30 USD) for a plate with sides. If you make it at home, the cost of ingredients will depend on the quality of the pork belly and apples you purchase, but it is typically a relatively inexpensive dish to make.

5 Low-Cost Denmark Hotel Options

1. Wakeup Copenhagen

Wakeup Copenhagen is a budget-friendly hotel chain that has multiple locations throughout Denmark. The hotels are designed with a modern and minimalist aesthetic, offering clean and comfortable rooms at a reasonable price. Wakeup Copenhagen has several different room types, ranging from single rooms to family rooms. Prices start at around 500 DKK (75 USD) per night for a single room, making it one of the most affordable hotel options in Denmark.

Wakeup Copenhagen also offers various amenities to make your stay more comfortable. Each room has a private bathroom and a flat-screen TV with cable channels. Free Wi-Fi is available throughout the hotel, and guests can purchase breakfast at an additional cost.

2. Cabinn City Hotel

Cabinn City Hotel is located in the heart of Copenhagen, making it an ideal choice for travelers who want to explore the city. The hotel offers simple yet comfortable accommodations at an affordable price. Cabinn City Hotel has several different room types, including single rooms, double rooms, and family rooms. Prices start at around 600 DKK (90 USD) per night for a single room.

Each room at Cabinn City Hotel has a private bathroom, a flat-screen TV, and free Wi-Fi. The hotel also offers a continental breakfast buffet at an additional cost. Cabinn City Hotel is within walking distance of many of Copenhagen's main attractions, including Tivoli Gardens and the Nyhavn waterfront.

3. Hotel Danmark

Hotel Danmark is located in the trendy Vesterbro neighborhood of Copenhagen. The hotel offers comfortable accommodations at a reasonable price, making it an excellent option for budget-conscious travelers. Hotel Danmark has several different room types, including single rooms, double rooms, and family rooms. Prices start at around 700 DKK (105 USD) per night for a single room.

Each room at Hotel Danmark is decorated in a modern Scandinavian style and has a private bathroom, a flat-screen TV, and free Wi-Fi. The hotel also has an on-site restaurant that serves traditional Danish cuisine. Guests can enjoy a continental breakfast buffet at an additional cost.

4. Hotel Domir

Hotel Domir is located in the charming town of Ribe, which is the oldest town in Denmark. The hotel is situated in a historic building and offers comfortable accommodations at an affordable price. Hotel Domir has several different room types, including single rooms, double rooms, and family rooms. Prices start at around 700 DKK (105 USD) per night for a single room.

Each room at Hotel Domir has a private bathroom, a flat-screen TV, and free Wi-Fi. The hotel also has an on-site restaurant that serves traditional Danish cuisine. Guests can enjoy a continental breakfast buffet at an additional cost. Hotel Domir is within walking distance of many of Ribe's main attractions, including the Ribe Cathedral and the Viking Museum.

5. Zleep Hotel Aarhus

Zleep Hotel Aarhus is located in the city of Aarhus, which is Denmark's second-largest city. The hotel offers simple yet comfortable accommodations at a reasonable price. Zleep Hotel

Aarhus has several different room types, including single rooms, double rooms, and family rooms. Prices start at around 700 DKK (105 USD) per night for a single room.

Each room at Zleep Hotel Aarhus has a private bathroom, a flat-screen TV, and free Wi-Fi. The hotel also has an on-site bar where guests can relax and socialize. A continental breakfast buffet is available at an additional cost.

Zleep Hotel Aarhus is located in a convenient location, within walking distance of many of the city's main attractions, such as the ARoS Aarhus Art Museum and the Aarhus Cathedral. The hotel is also located near several public transportation options, making it easy to explore the city.

5 Luxurious Places To Stay In Denmark

1) Hotel D'Angleterre, Copenhagen

Hotel D'Angleterre is a historic luxury hotel located in the heart of Copenhagen. The hotel dates back to 1755 and has been a beloved fixture in the city's social scene ever since. The hotel has been extensively renovated and modernized, while still retaining its classic charm and elegance.

Hotel D'Angleterre has several different room types, including deluxe rooms, junior suites, and grand suites. Prices start at around

4,500 DKK (680 USD) per night for a deluxe room. The rooms are decorated in a classic, sophisticated style and feature high-quality furnishings and luxurious amenities.

The hotel also has several on-site dining options, including the Michelin-starred restaurant Marchal. Guests can also enjoy the hotel's spa, which offers a range of treatments and wellness services.

2) Kokkedal Castle Copenhagen

Kokkedal Castle Copenhagen is a luxurious castle hotel located just outside of Copenhagen. The hotel is set on a stunning estate that includes a golf course, a lake, and beautiful gardens. The castle dates back to the 18th century and has been meticulously restored and renovated to offer modern comforts and amenities.

Kokkedal Castle Copenhagen has several different room types, including standard rooms, deluxe rooms, and suites. Prices start at around 2,500 DKK (380 USD) per night for a standard room. The rooms are decorated in a classic, elegant style and feature high-quality furnishings and luxurious amenities.

The hotel also has several on-site dining options, including the Michelin-starred restaurant Geranium. Guests can also enjoy the hotel's spa, which offers a range of treatments and wellness services.

3) Nimb Hotel, Copenhagen

Nimb Hotel is a luxurious boutique hotel located in Tivoli Gardens, one of Copenhagen's most popular attractions. The hotel is housed in a stunning historic building that dates back to 1909 and has been meticulously restored and renovated to offer modern comforts and amenities.

Nimb Hotel has several different room types, including standard rooms, deluxe rooms, and suites. Prices start at around 4,500 DKK (680 USD) per night for a standard room. The rooms are decorated in a sophisticated, modern style and feature high-quality furnishings and luxurious amenities.

The hotel also has several on-site dining options, including the Michelin-starred restaurant Almanak. Guests can also enjoy the hotel's spa, which offers a range of treatments and wellness services.

4) Kurhotel Skodsborg, Skodsborg

Kurhotel Skodsborg is a luxurious spa hotel located just outside of Copenhagen. The hotel is set in a beautiful location overlooking the Øresund Strait and has been a popular destination for wellness and relaxation for over 100 years.

Kurhotel Skodsborg has several different room types, including standard rooms, deluxe rooms, and suites. Prices start at around 2,500 DKK (380 USD) per night for a standard room. The rooms are decorated in a sophisticated, modern style and feature high-quality furnishings and luxurious amenities.

The hotel's spa is a highlight, offering a range of treatments and wellness services designed to promote relaxation and rejuvenation. The hotel also has several on-site dining options, including the Michelin-starred restaurant The Brasserie.

5)   Comwell Kellers Park, Brejning

Comwell Kellers Park is a luxurious spa hotel located in the scenic countryside of Brejning, just a short drive from the city of Vejle. The hotel is housed in a beautiful historic building that was once a spa resort and has been meticulously restored and renovated to offer modern comforts and amenities.

Comwell Kellers Park has several different room types, including standard rooms, deluxe rooms, and suites. Prices start at around 1,200 DKK (180 USD) per night for a standard room. The rooms are decorated in a classic, elegant style and feature high-quality furnishings and luxurious amenities.

The hotel's spa is a highlight, offering a range of treatments and wellness services designed to promote relaxation and rejuvenation.

The hotel also has several on-site dining options, including the Michelin-starred restaurant The Gourmet Room.

Top 5 Events in Sweden to Attend

1. Midsummer Festival

The Midsummer Festival is one of the most important and popular celebrations in Sweden. It takes place on the longest day of the year, usually around June 21st. This festival celebrates the arrival of summer and the coming of the light after the dark winter months. During the Midsummer Festival, people gather to dance around a maypole, sing traditional songs, and enjoy a traditional Swedish meal of pickled herring, potatoes, and strawberries.

If you attend the Midsummer Festival, you can experience the joy and excitement of this traditional Swedish celebration. You can participate in the dancing and singing, taste the delicious food, and learn about Swedish culture and traditions. The best time to attend the Midsummer Festival is during the summer months, usually between June and August.

2. Stockholm Pride

Stockholm Pride is an annual LGBT+ festival that takes place in Stockholm every summer. This festival is a celebration of diversity, equality, and love. During Stockholm Pride, people gather to participate in a range of activities, such as music concerts, art exhibitions, and parties. The highlight of the festival is the Pride Parade, which takes place in the center of Stockholm and attracts thousands of people from all over the world.

If you attend Stockholm Pride, you can experience the energy and excitement of this vibrant festival. You can enjoy the music, art, and parties, and celebrate love and diversity with people from all over the world. The best time to attend Stockholm Pride is in July, when the festival takes place.

3.   The Nobel Prize Ceremony

The Nobel Prize Ceremony is one of the most prestigious events takes place every year in Stockholm and is a celebration of excellence in science, literature, and peace activism. The ceremony is held at the Stockholm Concert Hall and is attended by the Swedish Royal Family, Nobel Laureates, and other dignitaries.

If you attend the Nobel Prize Ceremony, you can experience the elegance and prestige of this event. You can witness the awarding of one of the most prestigious honors in the world and learn about the groundbreaking work of the Nobel Laureates. The best time to attend the Nobel Prize Ceremony is in December, when the event takes place.

4.   The Göteborg Film Festival

The Göteborg Film Festival is the largest film festival in Scandinavia and takes place annually in Göteborg. This festival celebrates the best in Scandinavian and international cinema and offers a range of films, from feature-length dramas to short documentaries. The festival also includes workshops, seminars, and Q&A sessions with filmmakers and actors.

If you attend the Göteborg Film Festival, you can experience the excitement and creativity of this vibrant film festival. You can watch the latest Scandinavian and international films, meet filmmakers and actors, and participate in workshops and seminars. The best time to attend the Göteborg Film Festival is in January or February, when the festival takes place.

5.   The Vasaloppet Ski Race

The Vasaloppet Ski Race is one of the oldest and most prestigious ski races in the world. It takes place annually in Dalarna and is a tribute to the legendary Swedish king Gustav Vasa, who escaped from Danish captivity by skiing to safety in 1521. The race is 90 kilometers long and attracts thousands of skiers from all over the world.

If you attend the Vasaloppet Ski Race, you can experience the thrill and excitement of this legendary ski race. You can witness the determination and endurance of the skiers as they race through the beautiful Swedish countryside. The best time to attend the Vasaloppet Ski Race is in early March, when the race takes place.

Top 5 Must-Try Best Local Cuisine in Sweden

I.   Swedish Meatballs

Swedish meatballs are perhaps the most famous dish to come out of Sweden. They are traditionally made with a blend of ground pork and beef, mixed with breadcrumbs, eggs, and spices. The meatballs are then fried and served with lingonberry sauce, mashed potatoes, and pickled cucumbers.

The best place to try Swedish meatballs is at the legendary restaurant, Meatballs for the People. This restaurant is located in the trendy Södermalm district of Stockholm and offers a variety of meatball dishes, including traditional Swedish meatballs, as well as vegetarian and gluten-free options. Prices for a meal here can range from 150 SEK to 300 SEK per person.

II. Gravlax

Gravlax is a traditional Swedish dish made with salmon that has been cured with salt, sugar, and dill. The salmon is typically served cold and thinly sliced, and is often accompanied by a mustard and dill sauce.

The best place to try gravlax is at the famous restaurant, Lisa Elmqvist. Located in Stockholm's Östermalmshallen market hall, this restaurant has been serving traditional Swedish seafood dishes for over 80 years. A plate of gravlax at Lisa Elmqvist will cost you around 200 SEK.

III. Raggmunk

Raggmunk is a Swedish pancake made with grated potatoes and flour. The pancakes are typically served with fried pork and lingonberry jam.

The best place to try raggmunk is at Pelikan, a historic restaurant in Stockholm's trendy Södermalm district. Pelikan has been serving traditional Swedish cuisine since 1660, and is known for its hearty portions and cozy atmosphere. A plate of raggmunk at Pelikan will cost you around 200 SEK.

IV. Smörgåsbord

Smörgåsbord is a traditional Swedish buffet that features a variety of cold dishes, including pickled herring, smoked salmon, meatballs, and various salads.

The best place to try smörgåsbord is at the Grand Hôtel in Stockholm. The Grand Hôtel is one of Sweden's most luxurious hotels, and its smörgåsbord is considered to be one of the best in the country. Prices for a meal at the Grand Hôtel can range from 500 SEK to 800 SEK per person.

V. Fika

Fika is a Swedish tradition that involves taking a break from work or daily activities to enjoy a cup of coffee and a sweet treat. Fika can be enjoyed at any time of the day, and is often accompanied by a cinnamon bun, a piece of cake, or a small sandwich.

The best place to enjoy fika in Stockholm is at Vete-Katten, a traditional café that has been serving coffee and baked goods since 1928. Vete-Katten is known for its cozy atmosphere and delicious pastries, and a fika here will cost you around 50 SEK.

5 Low-Cost Sweden Hotel Options

1. Generator Stockholm

Located in the trendy Norrmalm district of Stockholm, Generator Stockholm is a stylish and affordable hostel that offers both private and shared accommodations. The hostel is housed in a converted 19th-century building and features a café, a bar, and a rooftop terrace with stunning views of the city. Prices for a bed in a shared dorm room start at around 250 SEK per night, while private rooms start at around 700 SEK per night.

2. STF City Hostel, Stockholm

STF City Hostel is a modern and affordable hostel located in the heart of Stockholm's city center. The hostel offers both private and shared accommodations, as well as a communal kitchen and lounge area. Prices for a bed in a shared dorm room start at around 250 SEK per night, while private rooms start at around 700 SEK per night.

3. Spar Hotel Gårdet, Gothenburg

Spar Hotel Gårdet is a budget-friendly hotel located in the quiet neighborhood of Gårdet in Gothenburg. The hotel offers simple yet comfortable accommodations, as well as a complimentary breakfast buffet. Prices for a double room start at around 600 SEK per night.

4. Ibis Styles Stockholm Odenplan

Ibis Styles Stockholm Odenplan is a modern and affordable hotel located in the Vasastan district of Stockholm. The hotel offers stylish and comfortable rooms, as well as a complimentary breakfast buffet. Prices for a double room start at around 800 SEK per night.

5. Scandic Triangeln, Malmö

Scandic Triangeln is a budget-friendly hotel located in the heart of Malmö. The hotel offers comfortable accommodations, as well as a complimentary breakfast buffet and access to a fitness center. Prices for a double room start at around 900 SEK per night.

5 Luxurious Places To Stay In Sweden

1) Grand Hotel Stockholm

Grand Hotel Stockholm is a luxurious five-star hotel located in the heart of Stockholm, overlooking the Royal Palace and the Old Town. The hotel is housed in a stunning 19th-century building and features lavish rooms and suites, a spa, several restaurants, and a rooftop bar with breathtaking views of the city. Prices for a deluxe room start at around 4,500 SEK per night, while a suite can cost up to 20,000 SEK per night.

2) Icehotel, Jukkasjärvi

Located in the small village of Jukkasjärvi in northern Sweden, Icehotel is a one-of-a-kind luxury hotel made entirely of ice and snow. Every winter, the hotel is rebuilt from scratch using blocks of ice from the nearby Torne River. The hotel features unique ice rooms, suites, and even a chapel, as well as warm accommodations for those who prefer to sleep in a more traditional room. Prices for an ice room start at around 7,500 SEK per night, while a suite can cost up to 25,000 SEK per night.

3) Treehotel, Harads

Treehotel is a unique and luxurious hotel located in the small village of Harads in northern Sweden. The hotel features several unique treehouses that are suspended high up in the trees and offer stunning views of the surrounding forest. Each treehouse is designed by a different architect and features unique themes, such as a UFO or a bird's nest. Prices for a treehouse start at around 5,000 SEK per night.

4) Falkenberg Strandbad

Falkenberg Strandbad is a luxurious spa hotel located on the west coast of Sweden, just a few steps away from the sandy beach. The hotel features elegant rooms and suites, a spa with several indoor and outdoor pools, a fitness center, and several restaurants. Prices for a double room start at around 2,500 SEK per night.

5) The Retreat Club, Öland

The Retreat Club is a luxurious wellness retreat located on the island of Öland, off the east coast of Sweden. The retreat features several villas and suites, each with its own private spa and outdoor hot tub. The property also features a main building with a restaurant, a spa, and several communal areas. Prices for a villa start at around 9,000 SEK per night.

Top 5 Events in Finland to Attend

I.   Midnight Sun Film Festival

The Midnight Sun Film Festival is an annual event held in Sodankylä, a small town located in Lapland, Northern Finland. This festival celebrates the art of cinema and attracts film enthusiasts from all over the world. The festival takes place during the summer solstice when the sun does not set, giving visitors the opportunity to enjoy 24 hours of sunlight.

At the Midnight Sun Film Festival, visitors can expect to watch a wide variety of films from around the world. The festival has a relaxed and intimate atmosphere, and there are plenty of opportunities to meet filmmakers, actors, and other industry professionals. There are also workshops, panel discussions, and other events that explore different aspects of filmmaking.

The Midnight Sun Film Festival takes place in late June, during the summer solstice.

II. Flow Festival

The Flow Festival is a three-day music festival that takes place in Helsinki every August. This festival is known for its diverse lineup, which includes international and Finnish musicians from a variety of genres. The festival takes place in Suvilahti, an industrial area that has been transformed into a vibrant cultural hub.

At the Flow Festival, visitors can expect to see some of the biggest names in music as well as up-and-coming artists. In addition to the music, there are also art installations, food vendors, and other activities to enjoy. The festival has a relaxed and laid-back atmosphere, and visitors can explore the different stages and areas at their own pace.

The Flow Festival takes place in August, during the summer.

III. Ruisrock

Ruisrock is Finland's oldest and largest rock music festival, held annually in Turku. This festival attracts tens of thousands of visitors each year and has featured some of the biggest names in rock and pop music.

At Ruisrock, visitors can expect to see a wide variety of musicians, from classic rock bands to modern pop artists. In addition to the music, there are also food vendors, merchandise booths, and other activities to enjoy. The festival has a lively atmosphere, and visitors can soak up the sun and enjoy the music with thousands of other fans.

Ruisrock takes place in July, during the summer.

IV. Helsinki Design Week

Helsinki Design Week is an annual event that celebrates design and creativity in all its forms. The event takes place in Helsinki and features a wide range of exhibitions, workshops, and other events that showcase the best in Finnish and international design.

At Helsinki Design Week, visitors can expect to see a wide variety of design exhibitions and installations, as well as attend workshops and talks by designers and other industry professionals. The event is a great opportunity to learn about Finnish design and discover new trends and ideas in the field.

Helsinki Design Week takes place in September.

Santa Claus Village

Santa Claus Village is a popular tourist destination located in Rovaniemi, Lapland. This village is known for its Christmas-themed attractions and is a great place to visit for families with children.

At Santa Claus Village, visitors can meet Santa Claus himself, as well as his elves and reindeer. There are also a variety of other activities to enjoy, such as sleigh rides, snowmobiling, and ice fishing. The village is a winter wonderland, with snow-covered landscapes and a magical atmosphere that will transport visitors to the North Pole.

Santa Claus Village is open year-round, but the best time to visit is during the winter months, from November to March.

Top 5 Must-Try Best Local Cuisine in Finland

1. Karjalanpiirakka

Karjalanpiirakka is a traditional Finnish pastry that originated in the region of Karelia. These small pies are made with a rye crust and filled with a mixture of rice or mashed potatoes.

Karjalanpiirakka is often served as a snack or appetizer and is a popular street food in Finland.

Karjalanpiirakka can be found at most bakeries and street food vendors in Finland. It is typically sold by the piece, and prices range from €1-€3 per pie.

2. Salmiakki

Salmiakki is a type of candy that is popular in Finland and other Nordic countries. This black licorice candy has a salty flavor and is made with ammonium chloride. Salmiakki comes in a variety of forms, including hard candies, gummies, and chocolate.

Salmiakki can be found at most grocery stores and convenience stores in Finland. Prices range from €1-€5 depending on the size and type of candy.

3. Kalakukko

Kalakukko is a traditional Finnish fish pie that originated in the region of Savonia. This hearty dish is made with rye dough and filled with a mixture of fish, bacon, and onions. Kalakukko is often served as a main course and is a popular dish during the summer months.

Kalakukko can be found at most restaurants and bakeries in Finland. It is typically sold by the slice, and prices range from €5-€10 per slice.

4. Lihapullat

Lihapullat, or Finnish meatballs, are a staple of Finnish cuisine. These small meatballs are made with a mixture of ground beef and pork and are often served with lingonberry jam and mashed potatoes. Lihapullat is a comforting and hearty dish that is popular throughout Finland.

Lihapullat can be found at most restaurants in Finland. They are typically served as a main course and prices range from €10-€20 depending on the restaurant.

5. Poronkäristys

Poronkäristys, or sautéed reindeer, is a traditional Finnish dish that is popular in Lapland. This hearty stew is made with tender reindeer meat and served with mashed potatoes, lingonberry jam, and pickles. Poronkäristys is a unique and delicious dish that is a must-try for visitors to Finland.

Poronkäristys can be found at most restaurants in Lapland. It is typically served as a main course and prices range from €20-€30 depending on the restaurant.

5 Low-Cost Finland Hotel Options

1)   Omena Hotel Helsinki Lonnrotinkatu

Located in the heart of Helsinki, the Omena Hotel Helsinki Lonnrotinkatu is a great option for budget-conscious travelers. The hotel offers simple, modern rooms that are perfect for those who just need a comfortable place to sleep. Each room features a kitchenette, free Wi-Fi, and a flat-screen TV. The hotel is just a short walk from many of Helsinki's top attractions, including the Helsinki Cathedral, the Senate Square, and the Market Square. Prices start at around 60 euros per night for a double room.

2) Hotel Arthur

Another great option in Helsinki is the Hotel Arthur. This historic hotel dates back to 1907 and offers a unique blend of old-world charm and modern amenities. The rooms are comfortable and well-appointed, with free Wi-Fi, flat-screen TVs, and minibars. The hotel also has a sauna and a fitness center, making it a great choice for those who want to stay active during their trip. The location is perfect for exploring the city, with many of Helsinki's top attractions just a short walk away. Prices start at around 80 euros per night for a double room.

3) Hostel Domus Academica

If you're looking for a more affordable option in Helsinki, the Hostel Domus Academica is a great choice. Located in the trendy Kallio district, this hostel offers simple, clean rooms at a very reasonable price. The rooms are basic, but they have everything you need, including free Wi-Fi and shared bathrooms. The hostel also has a communal kitchen and laundry facilities, making it a great option for budget-conscious travelers. The location is excellent, with many bars, restaurants, and shops within walking distance. Prices start at around 40 euros per night for a private room.

4)   Santa's Hotel Tunturi

If you're looking to explore Finland's stunning natural landscapes, the Santa's Hotel Tunturi is a great choice. Located in the town of Saariselkä in Finnish Lapland, this hotel offers cozy, rustic rooms that are perfect for those who want to experience the beauty of the Arctic wilderness. The hotel has a sauna and a hot tub, as well as a restaurant that serves traditional Finnish cuisine. The location is ideal for outdoor activities, with hiking, skiing, and snowshoeing opportunities right outside the door. Prices start at around 80 euros per night for a double room.

5)   Hostel Hullu Poro

Another great option in Lapland is the Hostel Hullu Poro, located in the town of Levi. This hostel offers simple, affordable rooms that are perfect for those who want to explore the Finnish wilderness on a budget. The rooms are basic, but they have everything you need, including free Wi-Fi and shared bathrooms. The hostel also has a communal kitchen and a sauna, making it a great option for those who want to relax after a day of outdoor activities. The location is ideal for winter sports, with skiing and snowboarding opportunities right outside the door. Prices start at around 40 euros per night for a private room.

5 Luxurious Places To Stay In Finland

1. Hotel Kämp, Helsinki

One of the most luxurious places to stay in Finland is the Hotel Kämp, located in the heart of Helsinki. This historic hotel has been a symbol of luxury and elegance since its opening in 1887. The rooms and suites at Hotel Kämp are beautifully appointed, with rich fabrics, plush furnishings, and all the modern amenities you could ask for. The hotel also features a spa, a fitness center, and a restaurant serving fine Finnish cuisine. Prices start at around 300 euros per night for a standard room and can go up to over 1000 euros per night for a luxurious suite.

2. Arctic TreeHouse Hotel, Rovaniemi

The Arctic TreeHouse Hotel in Rovaniemi offers a truly unique and luxurious experience. These stunningly designed, glass-walled accommodations are located in a forested area, providing breathtaking views of the surrounding nature. The rooms are stylishly furnished and feature all the modern amenities you could ask for, including a private sauna. The hotel also has a restaurant serving delicious Finnish cuisine, as well as a spa and wellness center. Prices start at around 500 euros per night for a standard room and can go up to over 1000 euros per night for a luxurious suite.

3.   Kakslauttanen Arctic Resort, Saariselkä

The Kakslauttanen Arctic Resort in Saariselkä is another luxurious option for those looking for a unique and unforgettable experience. The resort offers a range of accommodations, including glass igloos, log cabins, and traditional Finnish houses. The glass igloos are particularly popular, offering stunning views of the Northern Lights from the comfort of your own bed. The resort also features a restaurant serving delicious Finnish cuisine, as well as a spa and wellness center. Prices start at around 400 euros per night for a standard room and can go up to over 1000 euros per night for a luxurious suite.

4.   Levi Spirit Luxury Villas, Levi

The Levi Spirit Luxury Villas in Levi offer the ultimate in luxury and privacy. These luxurious villas are located in a peaceful forest setting, just a short drive from the ski resort of Levi. Each villa features a private sauna, a hot tub, a fireplace, and a fully equipped kitchen. The villas are beautifully designed and furnished, with all the modern amenities you could ask for. The resort also features a restaurant serving delicious Finnish cuisine, as well as a spa and wellness center. Prices start at around 500 euros per night for a standard villa and can go up to over 2000 euros per night for a luxurious villa.

5. Hotel Haven, Helsinki

Another luxurious option in Helsinki is the Hotel Haven. This elegant hotel is located in the historic district of Helsinki, just a short walk from the city's top attractions. The rooms and suites at Hotel Haven are beautifully designed and furnished, with all the modern amenities you could ask for. The hotel also features a spa and wellness center, a restaurant serving delicious Finnish cuisine, and a rooftop terrace with stunning views of the city. Prices start at around 300 euros per night for a standard room and can go up to over 1000 euros per night for a luxurious suite.

Top 5 Events in Iceland to Attend

I. Reykjavik Arts Festival

The Reykjavik Arts Festival is one of the most significant cultural events in Iceland, attracting artists, performers, and art enthusiasts from all over the world. The festival is held annually in late May and early June and features a wide range of art exhibitions, performances, and events. The festival's main goal is to promote contemporary art and culture in Iceland and to bring people together to celebrate creativity and diversity.

During the Reykjavik Arts Festival, visitors can expect to see a diverse range of art forms, including music, theater, dance, visual arts, and more. Many of the events take place in venues across

Reykjavik, such as the Harpa Concert Hall and the National Theatre of Iceland. The festival also includes outdoor performances and exhibitions, making it a great opportunity to explore the city and enjoy the beautiful Icelandic summer weather. The best time to attend the Reykjavik Arts Festival is in late May or early June, as this is when most of the events take place. Visitors should also book their accommodation well in advance, as the festival attracts a large number of people to the city.

Iceland Airwaves Music Festival

The Iceland Airwaves Music Festival is one of the most popular events in Iceland, attracting music lovers from all over the world. The festival is held annually in November and features a diverse range of musical genres, including rock, pop, electronic, and more. The festival's main goal is to promote Icelandic music and culture and to bring people together to celebrate creativity and diversity.

During the Iceland Airwaves Music Festival, visitors can expect to see a wide range of Icelandic and international artists performing in venues across Reykjavik. The festival also includes off-venue performances, which take place in bars, cafes, and other unconventional spaces around the city. This gives visitors a chance to explore Reykjavik and discover new music in unexpected places.

The best time to attend the Iceland Airwaves Music Festival is in November, as this is when most of the events take place. Visitors should also book their accommodation well in advance, as the festival attracts a large number of people to the city.

The Icelandic Horse Festival

The Icelandic Horse Festival is a unique event that celebrates the Icelandic horse, a breed that has been a part of Icelandic culture for over a thousand years. The festival is held annually in early August and features a wide range of horse-related events and activities, including horse shows, competitions, and demonstrations.

During the Icelandic Horse Festival, visitors can expect to see some of the most beautiful and well-trained Icelandic horses in the country. There are also opportunities to go horseback riding and to learn more about the history and culture of the Icelandic horse. The festival is a great opportunity to experience Icelandic culture and to get up close and personal with one of Iceland's most beloved animals.

The best time to attend the Icelandic Horse Festival is in early August, as this is when most of the events take place. Visitors should also book their accommodation well in advance, as the festival attracts a large number of people to the area.

The Northern Lights

The Northern Lights, or Aurora Borealis, is a natural phenomenon that can be seen in Iceland during the winter months. The Northern Lights are caused by pguides from the sun colliding with the Earth's atmosphere, creating a colorful display of lights in the sky. Iceland is one of the best places in the world to see the Northern Lights, as the country is located close to the Earth's magnetic poles, which makes it a prime location for viewing this stunning natural spectacle.

The best time to see the Northern Lights in Iceland is between September and April, when the nights are long and dark. Visitors can take d tours to some of the best spots for viewing the Northern Lights, such as Thingvellir National Park, where the lights can often be seen dancing across the sky. It is important to note that the Northern Lights are a natural phenomenon, and visibility can be affected by weather conditions and other factors, so it is always a good idea to check the forecast before planning a trip to see them.

The Icelandic National Day

The Icelandic National Day is celebrated annually on June 17th and marks the anniversary of Iceland's independence from Denmark in 1944. The day is a national holiday in Iceland and is celebrated with parades, concerts, and other events throughout the country.

During the Icelandic National Day, visitors can expect to see Icelandic flags and decorations all around the country, as well as people dressed in traditional Icelandic clothing. The day is a great opportunity to experience Icelandic culture and to learn more about the country's history and traditions.

The best time to attend the Icelandic National Day celebrations is on June 17th, as this is when most of the events take place. Visitors should also be aware that many businesses and attractions may be closed on this day, so it is important to plan ahead.

Top 5 Must-Try Best Local Cuisine in Iceland

- **Lamb Soup**

Lamb soup, or "kjötsúpa" in Icelandic, is a traditional Icelandic dish that is hearty and delicious. Made with lamb, potatoes, carrots, onions, and other vegetables, the soup is typically seasoned with thyme and served with a thick slice of homemade bread. The soup is a staple in Icelandic cuisine, and can be found at most restaurants and cafes throughout the country.

The cost of lamb soup varies depending on the location and the restaurant. On average, a bowl of lamb soup will cost around 2000-

3000 ISK (approximately $16-24 USD). Some popular places to try lamb soup include Svarta Kaffi in Reykjavik, Café Loki in Reykjavik, and Kaffi Hornid in Akureyri.

● **Skyr**

Skyr is a traditional Icelandic dairy product that has been a part of Icelandic cuisine for over a thousand years. Similar to yogurt, skyr is made by straining whey from milk to create a thick, creamy product that is high in protein and low in fat. Skyr is typically served as a dessert, topped with berries or other fruits, or used as a base for smoothies and other drinks.

The cost of skyr varies depending on the brand and the size of the container. On average, a small container of skyr will cost around 100-200 ISK (approximately $0.80-1.60 USD). Skyr can be found at most supermarkets and grocery stores throughout Iceland, including Bónus, Krónan, and Hagkaup.

● **Plokkfiskur**

Plokkfiskur, or "fish stew," is a traditional Icelandic dish that is made with fish, potatoes, and onions. The dish is typically seasoned with spices like bay leaves and black pepper, and served with rye bread and butter. Plokkfiskur is a comfort food in Iceland, and can be found at most restaurants and cafes throughout the country.

The cost of plokkfiskur varies depending on the location and the restaurant. On average, a serving of plokkfiskur will cost around 2000-3000 ISK (approximately $16-24 USD). Some popular places to try plokkfiskur include Kaffi Reykjavik in Reykjavik, Bryggjan Café in Akureyri, and Kaffi Hornid in Akureyri.

- **Fermented Shark**

Fermented shark, or "hákarl" in Icelandic, is a traditional Icelandic dish that is made from the meat of Greenland sharks. The shark meat is fermented for several months, then dried and cut into small cubes. The dish has a strong ammonia-like odor and a very strong taste, making it an acquired taste for most people.

The cost of fermented shark varies depending on the location and the restaurant. On average, a serving of fermented shark will cost around 2000-3000 ISK (approximately $16-24 USD). Fermented shark can be found at most restaurants and cafes throughout Iceland, although it is not a common menu item. Some popular places to try fermented shark include Islenski Barinn in Reykjavik and Fjöruborðið in Stokkseyri.

- **Grilled Lamb**

Grilled lamb, or "lamb on a stick," is a popular Icelandic dish that is simple but flavorful. The lamb is marinated in herbs and spices, then grilled over an open flame until it is tender and juicy. Grilled lamb is often served with potatoes and vegetables, and can be found at most restaurants and cafes throughout the country.

The cost of grilled lamb varies depending on the location and the restaurant. On average, a serving of grilled lamb will cost around 3000-5000 ISK (approximately $24-40 USD). Some popular places to try grilled lamb include Kex Hostel in Reykjavik, Roadhouse in Akureyri, and Sægreifinn in Reykjavik.

5 Low-Cost Iceland Hotel Options

1. Kex Hostel

Kex Hostel is located in the heart of Reykjavik and is a popular budget option for travelers. The hostel has a vintage-industrial design with a bar, restaurant, and communal spaces. The dormitory rooms have bunk beds and shared bathrooms, while the private rooms have en-suite bathrooms. The hostel also has a kitchen that guests can use to cook their own meals.

The cost of staying at Kex Hostel varies depending on the season and room type. A bed in a 16-bed dormitory room costs around

5,000 ISK (approximately $40 USD) per night, while a private double room with a shared bathroom costs around 20,000 ISK (approximately $160 USD) per night.

2. Hlemmur Square

Hlemmur Square is a budget hotel located in central Reykjavik. The hotel has a minimalist design with simple and modern rooms. The hotel has a bar and restaurant, and guests can enjoy free Wi-Fi and breakfast.

The cost of staying at Hlemmur Square varies depending on the season and room type. A standard double room costs around 20,000 ISK (approximately $160 USD) per night, while a single room costs around 10,000 ISK (approximately $80 USD) per night.

3. Reykjavik Hostel Village

Reykjavik Hostel Village is a budget-friendly hostel located in the trendy neighborhood of Laugardalur, just a short bus ride from Reykjavik city center. The hostel has dormitory rooms with bunk beds and shared bathrooms, as well as private rooms with en-suite bathrooms. The hostel also has a communal kitchen and lounge area, as well as a sauna and hot tub.

The cost of staying at Reykjavik Hostel Village varies depending on the season and room type. A bed in a 4-bed dormitory room costs around 4,000 ISK (approximately $32 USD) per night, while a private double room with a shared bathroom costs around 20,000 ISK (approximately $160 USD) per night.

4. Bus Hostel

Bus Hostel is located near Reykjavik's main bus terminal, making it a convenient budget option for travelers arriving in Iceland by bus. The hostel has dormitory rooms with bunk beds and shared bathrooms, as well as private rooms with en-suite bathrooms. The hostel also has a communal kitchen and lounge area.

The cost of staying at Bus Hostel varies depending on the season and room type. A bed in a 6-bed dormitory room costs around 5,000 ISK (approximately $40 USD) per night, while a private double room with a shared bathroom costs around 20,000 ISK (approximately $160 USD) per night.

5. Hotel Hilda

Hotel Hilda is a budget hotel located in central Reykjavik. The hotel has a cozy and modern design with simple and comfortable rooms. The hotel also has a communal lounge area, as well as a kitchenette with a microwave, fridge, and coffee maker that guests can use.

The cost of staying at Hotel Hilda varies depending on the season and room type. A standard double room costs around 20,000 ISK (approximately $160 USD) per night, while a single room costs around 14,000 ISK (approximately $112 USD) per night.

5 Luxurious Places To Stay In Iceland

1) The Retreat at Blue Lagoon

The Retreat at Blue Lagoon is a luxury hotel located in a geothermal spa resort in southwestern Iceland. The hotel has 62 rooms and suites with floor-to-ceiling windows that offer breathtaking views of the lagoon and surrounding lava fields. The rooms are elegantly decorated with natural materials like wood and stone, and feature modern amenities like heated floors and Nespresso machines. The hotel also has a restaurant, bar, and a spa with a variety of treatments and facilities, including a sauna, steam room, and a private lagoon.

The cost of staying at The Retreat at Blue Lagoon varies depending on the season and room type. A standard room costs around 99,000 ISK (approximately $800 USD) per night, while a suite costs around 170,000 ISK (approximately $1,380 USD) per night.

2) Hotel Rangá

Hotel Rangá is a luxury hotel located in the rural southern region of Iceland, near the famous Golden Circle route. The hotel has 51 rooms and suites with a rustic-chic design that reflects the surrounding countryside. The rooms feature modern amenities like flat-screen TVs and free Wi-Fi, as well as unique touches like Icelandic wool blankets and artwork. The hotel also has a restaurant that serves gourmet Icelandic cuisine, as well as a bar, a library, and a spa with a hot tub and sauna.

The cost of staying at Hotel Rangá varies depending on the season and room type. A standard room costs around 65,000 ISK (approximately $530 USD) per night, while a suite costs around 150,000 ISK (approximately $1,220 USD) per night.

3)   Ion Adventure Hotel

The Ion Adventure Hotel is a luxury hotel located on the edge of Thingvellir National Park, just a 45-minute drive from Reykjavik. The hotel has 45 rooms and suites with a modern and minimalist design that incorporates natural materials like lava rock and driftwood. The rooms feature amenities like flat-screen TVs, free Wi-Fi, and eco-friendly toiletries. The hotel also has a restaurant, a bar, and a spa with a hot tub, sauna, and a range of treatments.

The cost of staying at Ion Adventure Hotel varies depending on the season and room type. A standard room costs around 45,000 ISK (approximately $365 USD) per night, while a suite costs around 110,000 ISK (approximately $890 USD) per night.

4) Hotel Borg

Hotel Borg is a luxury hotel located in the heart of Reykjavik, in a historic building that dates back to the 1930s. The hotel has 99 rooms and suites that are decorated in a classic Art Deco style, with plush fabrics and elegant furnishings. The rooms feature amenities like flat-screen TVs, free Wi-Fi, and marble bathrooms. The hotel also has a restaurant, a bar, and a fitness center.

The cost of staying at Hotel Borg varies depending on the season and room type. A standard room costs around 45,000 ISK (approximately $365 USD) per night, while a suite costs around 195,000 ISK (approximately $1,580 USD) per night.

5) Deplar Farm

Deplar Farm is a luxury lodge located in the remote northern region of Iceland, surrounded by snow-capped mountains and pristine wilderness. The lodge has 13 rooms and suites with a contemporary design that blends seamlessly with the natural environment. The rooms feature amenities like heated floors, a hot tub, and views of the surrounding mountains. The lodge also has a restaurant that serves gourmet cuisine made with locally-sourced ingredients, as well as a bar, a spa with a sauna and steam room, and a range of outdoor activities, including heli-skiing, snowmobiling, and whale watching.

The cost of staying at Deplar Farm varies depending on the season and room type. A standard room costs around 1,625,000 ISK (approximately $13,200 USD) per night, while a suite costs around 2,800,000 ISK (approximately $22,800 USD) per night.

Top 5 Events in Norway to Attend

- **Bergen International Festival**

The Bergen International Festival is one of Norway's oldest and most prominent cultural festivals, featuring a wide range of performances, including music, dance, theatre, and art. This event takes place every year in May and June, attracting visitors from all over the world. Visitors can experience traditional Norwegian folk music and dance, as well as international acts from various genres. The festival also offers workshops and lectures, making it an enriching experience for all attendees.

- **Midnight Sun Marathon**

The Midnight Sun Marathon is a unique event that takes place every year in Tromsø, Norway, during the summer solstice in June.

This marathon is different from other marathons as it takes place in the middle of the night, under the light of the midnight sun. The route takes runners through beautiful coastal landscapes and mountains, offering breathtaking views of the Norwegian wilderness. Even if you are not a runner, the event is worth attending to experience the unique phenomenon of the midnight sun and witness the vibrant atmosphere of the marathon.

● **Olsokdagene**

Olsokdagene is an annual festival that takes place in Stiklestad, Norway, in July. This festival celebrates the Norwegian saint, St. Olav, who was instrumental in spreading Christianity in Norway. The festival includes historical reenactments, concerts, and a medieval market, offering visitors a glimpse into Norway's rich history and culture. The highlight of the event is the St. Olav's play, which tells the story of the saint's life and is performed in a magnificent outdoor amphitheatre.

● **Northern Lights Festival**

The Northern Lights Festival is an annual event that takes place in Tromsø, Norway, in January. The festival celebrates the natural wonder of the northern lights, offering visitors a chance to experience the magical phenomenon through various concerts, exhibitions, and workshops. Visitors can also participate in outdoor activities, such as dog sledding and snowmobiling, making it an excellent winter experience. The festival's highlight is the

Midnight Sun Concert, where musicians perform under the northern lights, creating a surreal atmosphere.

Oslo Jazz Festival

The Oslo Jazz Festival is an annual event that takes place in Oslo, Norway, in August. This festival is one of the most significant jazz events in Europe, featuring some of the world's most renowned jazz musicians. Visitors can experience a wide range of jazz styles, from traditional to avant-garde, performed in various venues throughout the city. The festival also includes workshops and lectures, making it a great learning opportunity for jazz enthusiasts.

Top 5 Must-Try Best Local Cuisine in Norway

I. Fårikål

Fårikål is Norway's national dish, and for a good reason. It's a hearty and delicious meal that's perfect for cold weather. Fårikål consists of lamb meat, cabbage, whole black pepper, and a touch of salt. The dish is boiled for several hours until the meat is tender and the flavors have melded together. Fårikål is typically served with boiled potatoes, lingonberry jam, and a glass of beer.

To try Fårikål, head to any traditional Norwegian restaurant or ask your hotel for recommendations. The dish is typically served in the fall when the lamb is at its best. Expect to pay around 200-300 NOK per serving, depending on the restaurant.

II. Kjøttkaker

Kjøttkaker is a traditional Norwegian meatball dish made with ground beef or pork, breadcrumbs, and a variety of spices. The meatballs are typically served with boiled potatoes, lingonberry jam, and gravy. Kjøttkaker is a hearty and filling meal that's perfect for any time of year.

To try Kjøttkaker, head to any traditional Norwegian restaurant or ask your hotel for recommendations. The dish is typically served all year round and can cost around 150-250 NOK per serving, depending on the restaurant.

III. Fiskesuppe

Fiskesuppe is a traditional Norwegian fish soup that's perfect for seafood lovers. The soup is made with a variety of fish such as cod, salmon, and haddock, along with vegetables like potatoes, carrots, and leeks. The dish is seasoned with a touch of cream, dill, and parsley, which gives it a rich and flavorful taste.

To try Fiskesuppe, head to any traditional Norwegian restaurant or ask your hotel for recommendations. The dish is typically served all year round and can cost around 150-250 NOK per serving, depending on the restaurant.

IV. **Lefse**

is a Norwegian flatbread that's often enjoyed as a snack or dessert. It's made from potatoes, flour, milk, and butter and is rolled thin and cooked on a griddle. Lefse can be served plain or with a variety of toppings such as butter, sugar, cinnamon, or lingonberry jam.

To try Lefse, head to a local bakery or cafe. Lefse is typically available all year round and is relatively inexpensive, costing around 20-40 NOK per piece.

V. **Krumkake**

Krumkake is a traditional Norwegian waffle cookie that's popular during the holidays. The cookie is made from flour, sugar, butter, and cream and is cooked on a special iron that gives it a decorative pattern. Krumkake is often filled with whipped cream or a sweet cheese filling and is served as a dessert.

To try Krumkake, head to a local bakery or cafe. Krumkake is typically only available during the holiday season and can cost around 20-40 NOK per piece.

Expenses

The cost of dining out in Norway can be quite expensive compared to other countries, but it's worth it to try the local cuisine. The cost of a meal can vary depending on the restaurant and location, but expect to pay around 150-300 NOK per dish. Drinks such as beer or wine can also be quite expensive, costing around 60-100 NOK per glass.

If you're on a budget, consider visiting local bakeries or cafes for a more affordable meal. Lefse and Krumkake are both relatively inexpensive and can be found at most bakeries for around 20-40 NOK per piece.

5 Low-Cost Norway Hotel Options

1. Citybox Oslo

Citybox Oslo is a budget-friendly hotel located in the heart of Oslo city, just a 2-minute walk from the Oslo Central Station. The hotel offers compact and functional rooms with a comfortable bed, flat-screen TV, and private bathroom. The rooms are designed to maximize space and minimize unnecessary amenities, resulting in lower prices without compromising on comfort. Guests can choose from three room categories - economy, standard, and superior, based on their preferences and budget.

The hotel also features a self-check-in system that allows guests to check-in and check-out at their convenience. Citybox Oslo has a 24-hour reception desk and a common lounge area where guests can relax, work, or socialize. The hotel does not offer breakfast, but there are several cafes and restaurants nearby that serve breakfast and other meals.

The price for an economy room starts at NOK 595 (approximately $68) per night, while the standard and superior rooms cost NOK 795 (approximately $91) and NOK 995 (approximately $114) per night, respectively.

2. Smarthotel Oslo

Smarthotel Oslo is another affordable hotel located in Oslo city, just a short walk from the Oslo Central Station and the main shopping street. The hotel offers modern and comfortable rooms with free Wi-Fi, flat-screen TV, and private bathroom. The rooms are small but functional, and feature bright and colorful interiors that create a cheerful and cozy atmosphere.

Smarthotel Oslo has a 24-hour reception desk and a self-check-in system that allows guests to check-in and check-out at their convenience. The hotel does not have a restaurant, but guests can enjoy a complimentary breakfast buffet served in the cozy breakfast lounge. The hotel also offers a vending machine that sells snacks and drinks.

The price for a standard room starts at NOK 699 (approximately $80) per night, while the superior room costs NOK 899 (approximately $103) per night.

3. Thon Hotel Sandnes

Thon Hotel Sandnes is a budget-friendly hotel located in Sandnes, a vibrant and charming city in southwestern Norway. The hotel offers modern and spacious rooms with free Wi-Fi, flat-screen TV, and private bathroom. The rooms are bright and stylish, with a minimalist and functional design that creates a peaceful and relaxing atmosphere.

Thon Hotel Sandnes has a 24-hour reception desk and a restaurant that serves breakfast, lunch, and dinner. The hotel also has a fitness center and a sauna that guests can use for free. The hotel is located in the city center, close to shops, restaurants, and attractions such as the Kongeparken amusement park and the stunning Lysefjorden. The price for a standard room starts at NOK 849 (approximately $97) per night, while the superior room costs NOK 999 (approximately $114) per night.

Comfort Hotel Xpress Central Station

Comfort Hotel Xpress Central Station is a budget-friendly hotel located in Bergen, a picturesque city on the southwestern coast of Norway. The hotel offers modern and colorful rooms with free Wi-Fi, flat-screen TV, and private bathroom. The rooms are designed to be functional and efficient, with adjustable beds and a smart TV that allows guests to stream their own content.

Comfort Hotel Xpress Central Station has a self-check-in system that allows guests to check-in and check-out at their convenience, and a 24-hour reception desk. The hotel does not have a restaurant, but guests can enjoy a complimentary breakfast buffet served in the cozy breakfast lounge. The hotel also has a lounge area where guests can relax, work, or socialize.

The hotel is located in the city center, just a short walk from the Bergen Central Station, the Fish Market, and other attractions such as the Fløibanen funicular and the Bryggen Hanseatic Wharf.
The price for a standard room starts at NOK 699 (approximately $80) per night, while the superior room costs NOK 849 (approximately $97) per night.

Thon Hotel Bergen Airport
Thon Hotel Bergen Airport is a budget-friendly hotel located in Bergen, just a short walk from the Bergen Airport. The hotel offers modern and comfortable rooms with free Wi-Fi, flat-screen TV, and private bathroom. The rooms are spacious and stylish, with a warm and welcoming atmosphere that creates a relaxing and comfortable stay.

Thon Hotel Bergen Airport has a 24-hour reception desk and a restaurant that serves breakfast, lunch, and dinner. The hotel also has a fitness center and a sauna that guests can use for free. The hotel is located near several attractions such as the Bergen Aquarium, the Edvard Grieg Museum Troldhaugen, and the Fantoft Stave Church.

The price for a standard room starts at NOK 849 (approximately $97) per night, while the superior room costs NOK 999 (approximately $114) per night.

5 Luxurious Places To Stay In Norway

1)   The Thief Hotel - Oslo

Located in Oslo, The Thief Hotel is a luxury boutique hotel that combines contemporary design with traditional Norwegian hospitality. The hotel features 118 rooms and suites, each uniquely decorated with high-quality furnishings and original artwork. The rooms offer breathtaking views of the Oslofjord or the city skyline and come with modern amenities such as flat-screen TVs, high-speed internet, and luxurious bedding.

The Thief Hotel offers a range of facilities, including a spa, fitness center, and a rooftop bar with panoramic views of the city. The hotel also has two restaurants - one serving traditional Norwegian cuisine, and the other offering a more international menu. Guests can also enjoy a complimentary breakfast buffet served in the hotel's restaurant.

The price for a standard room starts at NOK 3,295 (approximately $375) per night, while the suite costs NOK 8,995 (approximately $1,025) per night.

2)   The Britannia Hotel - Trondheim

The Britannia Hotel in Trondheim is a historic hotel that has recently undergone an extensive renovation, combining classic charm with modern luxury. The hotel features 257 elegant rooms and suites, each decorated with plush furnishings and modern amenities. The rooms offer views of the city or the Nidelva River and come with flat-screen TVs, high-speed internet, and luxurious bedding.

The Britannia Hotel offers a range of facilities, including a spa, fitness center, and a heated indoor pool. The hotel also has four restaurants, including a Michelin-starred restaurant, a brasserie, and a champagne bar. Guests can also enjoy a complimentary breakfast buffet served in the hotel's restaurant.

The price for a standard room starts at NOK 3,300 (approximately $376) per night, while the suite costs NOK 14,800 (approximately $1,685) per night.

3) The Storfjord Hotel - Stranda

The Storfjord Hotel is a luxurious mountain lodge located in Stranda, offering guests a unique and authentic Norwegian experience. The hotel features 29 rooms and suites, each decorated with natural materials and traditional Norwegian design elements. The rooms offer stunning views of the fjord or the surrounding mountains and come with modern amenities such as flat-screen TVs, high-speed internet, and luxurious bedding.

The Storfjord Hotel offers a range of facilities, including a spa, fitness center, and a hot tub with panoramic views of the mountains. The hotel also has a restaurant that serves traditional Norwegian cuisine made with local ingredients, as well as a bar and lounge area with a fireplace. Guests can also enjoy a complimentary breakfast served in the hotel's restaurant.

The price for a standard room starts at NOK 3,990 (approximately $454) per night, while the suite costs NOK 7,990 (approximately $910) per night.

4) The Juvet Landscape Hotel - Valldal

The Juvet Landscape Hotel is a luxurious hotel located in Valldal, offering guests a unique and immersive experience in nature. The hotel features nine detached rooms, each designed to blend seamlessly into the surrounding landscape. The rooms offer stunning views of the mountains, forest, or river and come with modern amenities such as flat-screen TVs, high-speed internet, and luxurious bedding.

The Juvet Landscape Hotel offers a range of facilities, including a spa, sauna, and outdoor hot tubs that allow guests to relax and enjoy the stunning natural surroundings. The hotel also has a restaurant that serves delicious meals made with locally-sourced ingredients, and a lounge area with a fireplace. Guests can also enjoy a complimentary breakfast served in the hotel's restaurant.

The price for a standard room starts at NOK 3,900 (approximately $444) per night, while the suite costs NOK 5,900 (approximately $672) per night.

The Farris Bad Hotel - Larvik

The Farris Bad Hotel is a luxurious spa hotel located in Larvik, offering guests a relaxing and rejuvenating experience. The hotel features 176 rooms and suites, each elegantly designed with modern furnishings and high-quality amenities. The rooms offer views of the sea or the surrounding landscape and come with flat-screen TVs, high-speed internet, and luxurious bedding.

The Farris Bad Hotel offers a range of facilities, including a spa, fitness center, and an indoor and outdoor pool. The hotel also has two restaurants, one serving Nordic cuisine and the other offering international dishes, as well as a bar and lounge area. Guests can also enjoy a complimentary breakfast buffet served in the hotel's restaurant.

The price for a standard room starts at NOK 3,750 (approximately $428) per night, while the suite costs NOK 9,500 (approximately $1,082) per night.

CHAPTER 6

TIPS AND CONSIDERATIONS

Entry requirement

Passport and Visa Requirements

The first and foremost requirement for entering any of the Scandinavian countries is a valid passport. The passport must be valid for at least three months from the date of entry into the country. If you are a citizen of a country within the European Union, you do not need a visa to enter Denmark, Norway, or Sweden. However, if you are a citizen of a non-EU country, you may need a visa.

The visa requirements for non-EU citizens differ depending on the country they wish to visit. Norway is a signatory to the Schengen Agreement, which means that it follows the same visa requirements as the other Schengen countries. Therefore, if you are a citizen of a non-EU country and wish to visit Norway, you must apply for a Schengen visa. This visa allows you to travel to any of the Schengen countries, including Denmark and Sweden, for up to 90 days within a 180-day period.

If you are a citizen of a non-EU country and wish to visit Denmark or Sweden, you must apply for a visa specifically for those countries. This visa allows you to enter Denmark or Sweden only and not any other Schengen country.

It is important to note that visa requirements can change from time to time, so it is essential to check the latest information from the embassy or consulate of the country you wish to visit.

COVID-19 Entry Requirements

Due to the COVID-19 pandemic, there are additional entry requirements for traveling to Scandinavia. These requirements vary depending on the country you wish to visit and are subject to change based on the prevailing situation.

- **Denmark**

If you wish to enter Denmark, you must provide proof of a negative COVID-19 test taken within 48 hours before arrival. You can also provide proof of vaccination or a previous COVID-19 infection, which exempts you from the testing requirement.

- **Norway**

If you wish to enter Norway, you must provide proof of a negative COVID-19 test taken within 24 hours before arrival. You must also complete a registration form and undergo another COVID-19 test upon arrival.

- **Sweden**

If you wish to enter Sweden, there are no COVID-19 testing or quarantine requirements for travelers from EU countries, including Norway and Denmark. However, if you are traveling from a non-EU country, you must provide proof of a negative COVID-19 test taken within 72 hours before arrival.

It is important to note that these requirements can change at any time, and it is essential to check the latest information from the embassy or consulate of the country you wish to visit.

Other Entry Requirements

Apart from passport and visa requirements and COVID-19 restrictions, there are other entry requirements that you should be aware of when traveling to Scandinavia.

- **Travel Insurance**

While not mandatory, it is highly recommended that you have travel insurance that covers medical emergencies, trip cancellations, and other unforeseen events. This insurance can help protect you from unexpected expenses and provide peace of mind during your trip.

- **Proof of Funds**

When entering Denmark, Norway, or Sweden, immigration officials may ask for proof of sufficient funds to cover your stay. This can include bank statements, credit card statements, or cash.

- **Customs and Immigration**

When entering Scandinavia, you will go through customs and immigration. You must declare any items that you are bringing into the country, including medications, food, and alcohol. Failure to declare these items can result in fines or even legal action.

You must also present a valid reason for your visit, such as tourism, business, or study. It is essential to have all necessary documents, such as hotel reservations, letters of invitation, or enrollment certificates, to support your reason for visiting.

Restricted and Prohibited Items

Scandinavian countries have strict regulations on what items can be brought into the country. Some items are restricted, meaning that they can be brought in but must be declared and may require additional paperwork or fees. Other items are prohibited, meaning that they cannot be brought into the country under any circumstances.

Restricted items can include firearms, certain types of medication, and certain food items. Prohibited items can include illegal drugs, counterfeit goods, and items that pose a threat to public safety, such as weapons or explosives.

It is essential to research the specific restrictions and prohibitions for the country you wish to visit before your trip to avoid any issues at customs.

Travel Insurance

Travel insurance is an essential component of any trip, including travel to Scandinavia. While it is not a requirement for entry, having travel insurance can provide peace of mind and financial protection in case of unexpected events during your trip. In this guide, we will discuss the importance of travel insurance for tourists visiting Scandinavia and what you should look for in a travel insurance policy.

Why You Need Travel Insurance for Scandinavia

Scandinavia is known for its natural beauty, rich history, and unique culture, making it a popular destination for tourists from all over the world. However, traveling to a foreign country always carries some level of risk, and unexpected events can happen, such as illnesses, accidents, or travel delays. Having travel insurance can help mitigate these risks and provide financial protection in case of emergencies.

1. Medical Coverage

One of the most important aspects of travel insurance is medical coverage. In Scandinavia, medical costs can be high, and without insurance, you could be facing a significant financial burden in case of an injury or illness. Travel insurance typically covers medical expenses, including hospitalization, emergency treatment, and repatriation, which can be especially important if you need to be transported back to your home country for treatment.

2. Trip Cancellation and Interruption

Another benefit of travel insurance is trip cancellation and interruption coverage. If you need to cancel or cut short your trip due to unforeseen circumstances, such as a medical emergency, natural disaster, or political unrest, travel insurance can help cover the costs of lost deposits, non-refundable flights, and other expenses.

3. Baggage and Personal Belongings

Travel insurance can also cover loss or damage to your baggage and personal belongings during your trip. This can include theft, damage during transport, or lost luggage. The insurance can help cover the cost of replacing the lost or damaged items, which can provide peace of mind and alleviate any financial strain.

4. Emergency Assistance

If you find yourself in an emergency situation while traveling in Scandinavia, travel insurance can provide emergency assistance. This can include 24/7 access to a hotline for medical and travel assistance, as well as emergency transportation or evacuation in case of a natural disaster or political unrest.

What to Look for in a Travel Insurance Policy

When choosing a travel insurance policy for your trip to Scandinavia, there are several factors to consider to ensure that you have adequate coverage for your needs.

1) Medical Coverage Limits

Check the medical coverage limits of the policy, including the maximum amount of coverage for emergency medical treatment, hospitalization, and medical evacuation. Make sure that the coverage limits are sufficient for the costs of medical care in Scandinavia.

2) Trip Cancellation and Interruption Coverage

Verify that the policy covers the cost of trip cancellation and interruption due to unforeseen circumstances, and check the specific circumstances covered under the policy, such as natural disasters or political unrest.

Baggage and Personal Belongings Coverage

Check the coverage limits for loss or damage to your baggage and personal belongings, as well as any exclusions or deductibles.

3) Emergency Assistance

Verify that the policy provides 24/7 access to a hotline for emergency medical and travel assistance, as well as coverage for emergency transportation or evacuation.

4)   Exclusions and Limitations

Read the policy carefully to understand any exclusions or limitations, such as pre-existing medical conditions, adventure activities, or high-value items.

5)   Cost

Consider the cost of the policy and compare it to the coverage and benefits provided. While the cheapest policy may be tempting, it may not provide adequate coverage for your needs.

Safety and Preparedness

●   Research the Destination

Before traveling to Scandinavia, it is important to research your destination. Find out about the local customs, laws, and weather conditions. This information will help you prepare for your trip and avoid any potential risks or hazards. Make sure to also research the local emergency services and know how to contact them in case of an emergency.

Pack Accordingly

The weather in Scandinavia can be unpredictable, so it is important to pack accordingly. Bring layers of clothing that can be easily removed or added as needed. Make sure to also pack waterproof gear, such as raincoats and umbrellas, as well as comfortable shoes for walking. If you plan on hiking or spending time in the great outdoors, bring appropriate gear, such as sturdy boots and a first-aid kit.

● **Keep Your Belongings Safe**

Scandinavia is generally a safe destination, but it is still important to keep your belongings safe. Make sure to keep your valuables, such as your passport, money, and credit cards, in a safe place, such as a hotel safe. When out and about, keep your bags and belongings close to you and be aware of your surroundings. Pickpocketing can occur in crowded areas, so be especially vigilant in tourist hotspots.

● **Stay Aware of Your Surroundings**

While Scandinavia is generally a safe destination, it is important to stay aware of your surroundings at all times. Avoid walking alone in poorly lit areas, especially at night. When in crowded areas, be aware of pickpocketing and keep your bags and belongings close to you. If you feel unsafe or uncomfortable, trust your instincts and leave the area.

● **Know the Emergency Numbers**

Make sure to know the emergency numbers in the country you are visiting. In Denmark, the emergency number is 112, while in Norway and Sweden, it is 113. If you need medical assistance, dial 112 or go to the nearest hospital. In case of a fire, dial 112 and evacuate the building immediately.

- **Be Prepared for Natural Disasters**

Scandinavia is prone to natural disasters, such as snowstorms and avalanches, especially during the winter months. If you plan on traveling during the winter, make sure to check weather reports and road conditions before embarking on your journey. Bring appropriate gear, such as snow chains, and drive carefully. If you get caught in a snowstorm, stay in your car and wait for assistance.

If you plan on hiking or spending time in the great outdoors, make sure to check for any warnings or restrictions before embarking on your journey. Pay attention to weather reports and be prepared for sudden changes in weather conditions. Bring appropriate gear, such as a first-aid kit, and let someone know where you are going and when you plan on returning.

- **Stay Informed about COVID-19**

Like many other destinations around the world, Scandinavia has been affected by the COVID-19 pandemic. Make sure to stay informed about any travel restrictions, quarantine measures, and health lines in place in the country you are visiting. Check with your airline or travel agent for the latest information and make sure to follow any lines in place to protect yourself and others.

Money Matters And Saving Tips

1. Currency and Exchange Rates

The currency in Denmark is the Danish Krone (DKK), in Norway it is the Norwegian Krone (NOK), and in Sweden it is the Swedish Krona (SEK). While credit cards are widely accepted, it is a good idea to have some cash on hand for smaller purchases and to avoid currency exchange fees. Before your trip, check the exchange rate and compare rates from different exchange providers to ensure you get the best deal.

2. Budgeting and Planning

Before embarking on your trip to Scandinavia, it is important to set a realistic budget and plan your expenses accordingly. Take into account the cost of transportation, accommodations, food, activities, and souvenirs. Research prices and make reservations in advance to get the best deals. Consider traveling during the shoulder season, which is typically less crowded and less expensive than peak season.

3. Accommodation Options

Accommodation can be one of the biggest expenses when traveling to Scandinavia. Consider alternative options such as hostels, guesthouses, and Airbnb rentals. These options can be significantly cheaper than hotels and offer a more authentic experience. However, make sure to read reviews and check the location before booking to ensure the accommodation is safe and meets your needs.

4. Transportation

Public transportation is a cost-effective way to get around Scandinavia. Trains and buses are widely available and are often cheaper than renting a car. Consider purchasing a travel pass, which can provide unlimited access to public transportation and save you money in the long run. If you do decide to rent a car, make sure to shop around for the best deal and read the fine print before signing the contract.

5. Food and Drinks

Eating out in Scandinavia can be expensive, especially in tourist areas. Consider cooking some meals yourself if you have access to a kitchen. Grocery stores in Scandinavia offer a wide selection of fresh and affordable produce, meat, and dairy products. Make use of the free water fountains available in public areas to avoid buying bottled water, which can be expensive.

If you do decide to eat out, consider ordering a lunch menu instead of a dinner menu. Lunch menus are often cheaper and offer a similar selection of dishes. Look for restaurants that offer early bird or happy hour specials, which can be a great way to save money on drinks and food.

6. Activities and Sightseeing

Scandinavia offers a wide range of activities and sightseeing opportunities, but they can come at a cost. Look for free or low-cost activities, such as visiting parks and museums, taking a walking tour, or exploring the local markets. Check for discounts and coupons online or at tourist information centers. Consider purchasing a city pass or museum pass, which can provide discounts on admission fees and transportation.

7. Shopping and Souvenirs

Shopping in Scandinavia can be expensive, especially for designer brands and high-end products. Consider purchasing souvenirs from local markets and independent shops instead of tourist shops. Look for handmade or locally produced items, which can offer a more authentic and unique experience. Keep in mind that some items, such as alcohol and tobacco products, may be subject to taxes and customs fees when returning home.

8. Saving Money on Flights

Flights to Scandinavia can be expensive, but there are ways to save money. Consider traveling during the shoulder season, which is typically less crowded and less expensive than peak season. Book your flight well in advance and be flexible with your travel dates. Check for discounts and deals online or sign up for email alerts from airlines or travel booking websites to stay informed about promotions and sales.

Another option is to use travel rewards or points to book your flight. Many credit cards offer travel rewards programs that allow you to earn points or miles for every dollar spent on purchases.

These points can then be redeemed for flights, hotels, or other travel expenses. However, make sure to read the terms and conditions carefully, as some rewards programs may have blackout dates or restrictions on how points can be used.

9. Saving Money on Communication

Staying connected with friends and family back home can be expensive when traveling abroad. However, there are ways to save money on communication costs. Consider purchasing a local SIM card or using a mobile app that allows for free or low-cost international calling and messaging. Many coffee shops and public areas in Scandinavia offer free Wi-Fi, so take advantage of these to stay connected without incurring additional costs.

10. Tips for Using Credit Cards

Credit cards are widely accepted in Scandinavia, but it is important to be aware of potential fees and charges. Some credit cards charge foreign transaction fees, which can add up quickly when making purchases abroad. Look for credit cards that offer no foreign transaction fees or consider using a prepaid travel card instead.

It is also important to inform your bank and credit card company of your travel plans before leaving. This can help prevent your card from being flagged for fraud and ensure that you have access to your funds while abroad.

11. Safety Tips for Money Matters

Scandinavia is generally a safe destination for tourists, but it is still important to take precautions when it comes to money matters. Keep your valuables, such as cash, credit cards, and passport, in a secure place, such as a hotel safe or a money belt. Avoid carrying large amounts of cash and be aware of your surroundings when using ATMs or making purchases.

It is also a good idea to carry a backup credit card or cash in case of emergencies. Make copies of important documents, such as your passport and travel insurance policy, and keep them in a separate location from the originals.

Local Customs and Etiquette

When traveling to Scandinavia, it is important to be aware of local customs and etiquette to ensure a positive and respectful experience. While the Scandinavian countries share many cultural similarities, there are also some notable differences in customs and social norms that visitors should be aware of.

Greeting Customs

In Scandinavia, greetings are generally reserved and formal. Handshakes are the most common form of greeting, but it is important to wait for the other person to initiate the handshake before extending your hand. In Norway and Sweden, it is also common to exchange a quick hug or kiss on the cheek with close friends and family members.

When addressing someone, it is common to use their title and last name, such as "Mr. Johnson" or "Ms. Anderson." Using first names is generally reserved for close friends and family members.

Socializing Customs

Socializing is an important part of Scandinavian culture, but it is important to be aware of local customs and social norms when interacting with locals. In general, Scandinavians value their personal space and tend to be reserved and polite in social situations.

When invited to someone's home for dinner or a social gathering, it is important to arrive on time or a few minutes early. Bringing a small gift, such as flowers or chocolates, is also a common custom in Scandinavia.

When socializing in a group, it is important to take turns speaking and avoid interrupting others. Scandinavians value directness and honesty, so it is important to be clear and straightforward in your communication.

Dining Customs

Dining customs in Scandinavia vary by country, but there are some general customs and etiquette rules to be aware of. In general, meal times tend to be formal and reserved, and it is common to wait until everyone is seated and served before starting to eat.

In Norway and Sweden, it is customary to raise a glass and make a toast before beginning the meal. It is also important to use utensils properly and avoid placing elbows on the table.

When finished with your meal, it is customary to place your knife and fork parallel on your plate, with the handles facing to the right. In Denmark, it is also customary to push your plate away from you when finished, while in Sweden and Norway, it is polite to leave your plate where it is.

Business Customs

In business settings, it is important to be aware of local customs and etiquette to ensure a positive and respectful experience. In general, Scandinavians value punctuality, honesty, and directness in business interactions.

When greeting someone in a business setting, it is important to use their title and last name, such as "Mr. Hansen" or "Ms. Olsen." Dressing professionally and conservatively is also important in business settings.

When conducting business negotiations, it is important to be straightforward and honest in your communication. Scandinavians value consensus and collaboration, so it is important to be respectful of others' opinions and work towards a common goal.

Public Customs

In public settings, it is important to be respectful of local customs and etiquette to avoid offending others. In general, Scandinavians value personal space and tend to be reserved in public.

When using public transportation, it is important to respect others' personal space and avoid speaking loudly or causing a disturbance. In general, it is also important to avoid littering or engaging in other disruptive behavior in public areas.

When visiting religious sites, it is important to dress modestly and avoid taking photos or engaging in other disrespectful behavior. In general, it is important to be respectful of local customs and traditions when visiting public areas and interacting with locals.

What to Do and What Not to Do When Visiting Scandinavia

- **Do: Embrace the Outdoors**

Scandinavia is home to some of the most breathtaking natural landscapes in the world, from Norway's fjords to Sweden's forests and Finland's lakes. Take advantage of the opportunity to explore the outdoors and engage in activities such as hiking, skiing, and kayaking. Scandinavians value their connection to nature and the outdoors, so immersing yourself in these experiences can also help you better understand the local culture.

- **Don't: Ignore the Environment**

While enjoying the outdoors, it is important to respect the environment and leave no trace behind. Scandinavians place a high value on sustainability and environmental stewardship, and littering or damaging natural resources is considered disrespectful and harmful. Be sure to dispose of waste properly, stay on designated trails, and follow other environmental lines to help protect these valuable resources for generations to come.

- **Do: Try the Local Cuisine**

Scandinavian cuisine is a unique and delicious blend of traditional dishes and modern culinary trends. From Swedish meatballs to Norwegian salmon and Danish pastries, there are plenty of mouthwatering options to explore. Trying local cuisine is also a great way to connect with locals and learn more about the history and culture of the region.

- **Don't: Insist on Familiar Foods**

While it is natural to crave familiar foods while traveling, it is important to avoid being too picky or insisting on foods that are not common in the region. Scandinavian cuisine may include ingredients or preparation methods that are different from what you are used to, but being open-minded and willing to try new things is part of the adventure of travel.

● **Do: Respect Local Customs and Etiquette**

As mentioned earlier, Scandinavia has its own unique customs and social norms that visitors should be aware of. It is important to be respectful of these traditions and act accordingly in social situations. This may include being reserved in public, using formal greetings and titles, and avoiding sensitive topics in conversation.

● **Don't: Be Disrespectful or Offensive**

While it is natural to have questions or opinions about local customs and traditions, it is important to avoid being disrespectful or offensive. This includes avoiding derogatory language, making assumptions about cultural practices, or engaging in behavior that may be considered inappropriate or offensive. Remember that you are a guest in someone else's home and showing respect is crucial for a positive and respectful experience.

● **Do: Learn About the History and Culture**

Scandinavia has a rich and fascinating history and cultural heritage. Taking the time to learn about the region's history, art, and literature can provide a deeper understanding and appreciation of the culture. Museums, historical sites, and cultural festivals are great opportunities to immerse yourself in the local culture and learn something new.

- **Don't: Stereotype or Generalize**

While it is natural to have preconceived notions or stereotypes about a particular culture or region, it is important to avoid generalizing or making assumptions. Each country and community within Scandinavia has its own unique identity and culture, and it is important to approach each experience with an open mind and willingness to learn.

By following these do's and don'ts, you can ensure a positive and respectful experience while visiting Scandinavia. Remember to stay curious, respectful, and open-minded, and enjoy all the region has to offer.

CHAPTER 7

UNDERSTANDING FOREIGN TRANSACTION FEES

Avoid Cell Phone Roaming Charges

If you're planning to visit Scandinavia as a tourist, you may be concerned about the potential for expensive cell phone roaming charges. Fortunately, there are several steps you can take to avoid these charges and stay connected during your trip.

First and foremost, it's important to understand what cell phone roaming charges are and how they work. When you use your cell phone outside of your home country, your carrier may charge you extra fees for using their network to make calls, send texts, or use data. These fees can add up quickly and can be especially expensive in countries like Denmark, Norway, and Sweden.

One of the best ways to avoid cell phone roaming charges is to use a local SIM card. A SIM card is a small chip that stores your cell phone's information and allows it to connect to a network. When you use a local SIM card, you're essentially using a different carrier's network, which can often be much cheaper than using your home carrier's network.

To use a local SIM card, you'll need to have an unlocked cell phone. This means that your phone isn't tied to a specific carrier and can be used with any SIM card. If your phone is locked, you may need to contact your carrier to have it unlocked before you can use a local SIM card.

Once you have an unlocked phone, you can purchase a local SIM card when you arrive in Scandinavia. You can often find SIM cards at airports, convenience stores, or cell phone shops. Make sure to compare prices and plans before you make a purchase, as prices can vary widely depending on the carrier and the plan you choose.

Another option is to rent a portable Wi-Fi hotspot. A hotspot is a small device that allows you to connect to the internet using a Wi-Fi connection. When you rent a hotspot, you'll be given a device that you can carry with you wherever you go, and you can connect your phone, tablet, or laptop to the hotspot to access the internet.

Renting a hotspot can be a good option if you don't want to switch SIM cards or if you need to connect multiple devices to the internet. However, it can be more expensive than using a local SIM card, so make sure to compare prices before you make a decision.

If you don't want to use a local SIM card or rent a hotspot, you can also try to limit your cell phone usage while you're in Scandinavia. This may mean using your phone only when you have access to Wi-Fi, or only using it for emergencies or important calls.

You can also turn off data roaming on your phone to prevent it from automatically connecting to a network when you're outside of your home country. This can help you avoid unexpected charges, but it also means that you won't be able to use data or make calls unless you're connected to Wi-Fi.

Before you travel to Scandinavia, make sure to check with your carrier to see what their international rates are. Some carriers offer international plans or packages that can help you save money on roaming charges, so it's worth looking into these options before you go.

You may also want to consider using messaging apps like WhatsApp or iMessage to stay in touch with friends and family while you're abroad. These apps allow you to send messages and make calls over the internet, so you won't need to use your cell phone network.

In addition to these options, there are a few other things you can do to avoid cell phone roaming charges in Scandinavia. Here are a few tips to keep in mind:

Turn off automatic updates and push notifications on your phone to prevent it from using data in the background.

Download maps and other travel information before you go so that you don't need to use data to access them while you're abroad.

Use public Wi-Fi networks when you can However, it's important to note that public Wi-Fi networks can be unsecured and may put your personal information at risk. To protect your privacy and security, make sure to use a virtual private network (VPN) when you connect to public Wi-Fi.

A VPN is a service that encrypts your internet connection and routes it through a secure server, making it much harder for anyone to intercept your data. There are many VPN services available, some of which are free and some of which require a subscription.

When you're using your cell phone in Scandinavia, it's also important to be mindful of your data usage. Even if you're using a local SIM card or renting a hotspot, data can still be expensive and can add up quickly.

To minimize your data usage, try to use Wi-Fi whenever possible. You can also turn off automatic app updates and background app refresh to prevent your phone from using data without your knowledge.

If you do need to use data while you're in Scandinavia, make sure to monitor your usage and avoid downloading large files or streaming videos. You can also use data compression apps like Opera Mini or Google Data Saver to reduce the amount of data that your phone uses.

Finally, if you're traveling with a group, consider using messaging apps or social media to communicate with each other instead of making individual phone calls or sending text messages. This can help you save money on roaming charges and can also make it easier to coordinate your plans and stay in touch.

Consider An Scandinavia Sim Card Or Mifi Device

Advantages of a Local SIM Card

The main advantage of getting a local SIM card is that it can be much cheaper than using your home carrier's international roaming plan. This is because local carriers often offer better rates for calls, texts, and data than international carriers.

Another advantage of getting a local SIM card is that it can be more convenient than using a MiFi device. With a local SIM card, you can simply pop it into your phone and start using it immediately, without having to carry around another device. This can be especially useful if you are planning to use your phone for navigation or other purposes throughout your trip.

Disadvantages of a Local SIM Card

One of the main disadvantages of getting a local SIM card is that you may have to unlock your phone first. This is because most phones are locked to a specific carrier, and in order to use a local SIM card, you will need to unlock your phone first. This can be a complicated process, and it may require you to contact your home carrier to request an unlock code.

Another disadvantage of getting a local SIM card is that you may not have coverage everywhere you go. This is because local carriers may not have the same level of coverage as international carriers, especially in rural or remote areas. This can be a problem if you need to stay connected for work or other important purposes.

Advantages of a MiFi Device

The main advantage of getting a MiFi device is that it can provide a more stable and reliable connection than a local SIM card. This is because a MiFi device acts as a mobile hotspot, allowing you to connect multiple devices to the internet at once. This can be especially useful if you are traveling with friends or family and need to stay connected to the internet at all times.

Another advantage of getting a MiFi device is that you can use it to connect other devices, such as laptops or tablets, to the internet. This can be useful if you need to work or stream content on a larger screen.

Disadvantages of a MiFi Device

One of the main disadvantages of getting a MiFi device is that it can be more expensive than getting a local SIM card. This is because you will need to pay for the device itself, as well as a data plan. However, if you plan to use a lot of data, a MiFi device may actually be cheaper in the long run, as you can often get better rates for larger data packages.

Another disadvantage of getting a MiFi device is that it can be more cumbersome to carry around than a local SIM card. This is because you will need to carry around the device itself, as well as any charging cables or adapters that you may need. This can be a problem if you are trying to pack light or are already carrying a lot of other devices with you.

Tips for Choosing the Best Plan

If you decide to get a local SIM card or a MiFi device, there are a few things to keep in mind when choosing a plan:

- **Consider your data usage:** Think about how much data you will need for your trip. If you plan to use a lot of data, a MiFi device may be a better option, as you can often get better rates for larger data packages. If you only need a small amount of data, a local SIM card may be more cost-effective.

- **Check coverage:** Make sure to check the coverage maps for the carriers you are considering. This is especially important if you plan to travel to remote areas or outside of major cities. You want to make sure that you have coverage wherever you go so that you can stay connected to the internet and your phone network.

- **Compare prices:** Compare the prices of different carriers and plans to find the best deal for your needs. Consider the cost of the device or SIM card, as well as the cost of the data plan. Don't forget to factor in any activation fees, taxes, or other charges that may apply.

- **Look for discounts:** Some carriers may offer discounts for tourists or for those who purchase their plans online. Check for any promotions or discounts that may apply to you.

- **Check the validity period:** Local SIM cards and MiFi devices usually have a limited validity period, after which you will need to renew your plan or purchase a new device. Make sure to check the validity period before you make your purchase, and consider how long you will be in Scandinavia.

- **Check the terms and conditions:** Read the terms and conditions of the carrier carefully before making your purchase. Make sure you understand any limitations or restrictions that may apply to your plan, such as data caps, speed restrictions, or roaming charges.

Download Offline Map

As a tourist, one of the most important things to have on hand while exploring a new destination is a reliable map. In today's digital age, maps are easily accessible through smartphone apps, and downloading an offline map can be incredibly beneficial, especially when exploring a new destination such as Scandinavia. In this guide, we will discuss the benefits of downloading an offline map for Scandinavia, the best apps to use, and how to get the most out of your offline map.

Benefits of Downloading an Offline Map

Downloading an offline map for Scandinavia can provide several benefits for tourists, including:

- **No need for internet:** One of the biggest benefits of downloading an offline map is that you do not need to be connected to the internet to use it. This is especially important when traveling in areas with limited or no internet access, or when you do not have access to an affordable data plan. With an offline map, you can navigate your way around Scandinavia without worrying about data charges or poor connectivity.

- **Save battery life:** Using online maps can quickly drain your phone's battery, especially if you are constantly checking your location and navigating through unfamiliar streets. An offline map can help to conserve your phone's battery life as it does not require constant internet connection and data usage.

- **Avoid getting lost:** With an offline map, you can easily navigate your way around Scandinavia, even when you are in areas with poor signal coverage or no internet access. You can view your current location, track your progress, and plan your route without the risk of getting lost.

- **Access to local recommendations:** Many offline map apps offer recommendations for local attractions, restaurants, and other places of interest. By using an offline map, you can discover new places to visit and experience the local culture.

Best Apps to Use

There are several offline map apps available that offer detailed maps of Scandinavia. Some of the best apps to use include:

- **Maps.me:** Maps.me is a popular offline map app that provides detailed maps of Scandinavia. The app offers turn-by-turn directions, local recommendations, and the ability to bookmark favorite locations. Maps.me also allows users to search for specific addresses and points of interest, making it easy to find your way around.

- **Google Maps:** Google Maps offers an offline feature that allows you to download maps for a specific region or city. Once downloaded, you can access the map without internet connection. Google Maps also offers local recommendations, public transit information, and the ability to search for specific addresses and points of interest.

- **CityMaps2Go:** CityMaps2Go offers detailed maps of Scandinavia, as well as local recommendations and the ability to search for specific addresses and points of interest. The app also offers a trip planning feature, allowing users to plan their itinerary and save their favorite locations.

- **OsmAnd:** OsmAnd is an open-source map app that offers offline maps of Scandinavia, as well as turn-by-turn directions and the ability to search for specific addresses and points of interest. The app also offers local recommendations, public transit information, and the ability to save favorite locations.

Getting the Most Out of Your Offline Map

To get the most out of your offline map, consider the following tips:

- **Download the map before you travel:** Make sure to download the offline map for Scandinavia before you travel. This will ensure that you have access to the map even if you do not have internet connection.

- **Update the map regularly:** Offline maps are often updated to include new locations, attractions, and road networks. Make sure to update the map regularly to ensure that you have the most up-to-date information.

- **Plan your route in advance:** Before setting out on your trip, plan your route in advance using the offline map. This will help you to navigate your way around Scandinavia more efficiently and avoid getting lost. You can also save favorite locations on the map for quick and easy access.

- **Use GPS sparingly:** GPS can quickly drain your phone's battery, so use it sparingly. Instead, try to navigate using the map and your own sense of direction. If you do need to use GPS, consider turning it off when you are not actively using it.

- **Check for local recommendations:** Many offline map apps offer local recommendations for attractions, restaurants, and other places of interest. Check these recommendations regularly to discover new and interesting places to visit.

- **Be aware of data usage:** While offline maps do not require internet connection, they may use data for certain features such as searching for specific addresses or points of interest. Make sure to monitor your data usage to avoid exceeding your data limit.

Learn Basic Language

Learning a basic language while traveling can greatly enhance your travel experience, particularly in Scandinavia, where the native languages may be unfamiliar to non-native speakers. While English is widely spoken in Scandinavia, learning a few basic words and phrases in the local languages can help you to connect with the locals and show respect for their culture. In this guide, we will discuss the benefits of learning a basic language in Scandinavia, the best ways to learn, and some essential phrases to get you started.

Benefits of Learning a Basic Language

Learning a basic language in Scandinavia can provide several benefits for tourists, including:

- **Connection with locals**: Learning a few basic words and phrases in the local language can help you to connect with locals on a more personal level. This can lead to more meaningful interactions and a better understanding of the local culture.

- **Respect for culture:** Learning the local language also shows respect for the local culture. Locals appreciate when visitors make an effort to speak their language, even if it is only a few basic words.

- **Better travel experience:** Knowing a basic language can also make your travel experience more enjoyable and less stressful. You can navigate your way around more easily, order food, ask for directions, and understand signs and announcements.

Best Ways to Learn

There are several ways to learn a basic language in Scandinavia, including:

- **Language classes:** You can take language classes in person or online before you travel to Scandinavia. This will give you a solid foundation in the language and allow you to practice with a teacher or tutor.

- **Language exchange:** You can find language exchange partners online or in person to practice speaking the language with a native speaker. This is a great way to improve your conversational skills and learn more about the local culture.

- **Language apps:** There are many language learning apps available, such as Duolingo, Babbel, and Rosetta Stone. These apps offer interactive lessons, vocabulary building exercises, and speech recognition technology to help you practice speaking.

- **Language books and audio resources:** You can also use language books and audio resources to learn the basics of the language. These resources include phrasebooks, language dictionaries, and audio s.

Essential Phrases to Get You Started

Here are some essential phrases to get you started when learning a basic language in Scandinavia:

1. Hello: Hej (Swedish), Hallo (Danish), Hei (Norwegian), Halló (Icelandic), Moi (Finnish)

2. Goodbye: Adjö (Swedish), Farvel (Danish), Ha det (Norwegian), Bless (Icelandic), Moikka (Finnish)

3. Thank you: Tack (Swedish), Tak (Danish), Takk (Norwegian), Takk fyrir (Icelandic), Kiitos (Finnish)

4. Please: Snälla (Swedish), Vær så snill (Danish), Vær så snill (Norwegian), Vinsamlegast (Icelandic), Ole hyvä (Finnish)

5. Yes: Ja (Swedish, Danish, Norwegian), Já (Icelandic), Kyllä (Finnish)

6. No: Nej (Swedish, Danish), Nei (Norwegian, Icelandic), Ei (Finnish)

7. Excuse me: Ursäkta (Swedish), Undskyld (Danish), Unnskyld (Norwegian), Fyrirgefðu (Icelandic), Anteeksi (Finnish)

8. Where is...?: Var är...? (Swedish), Hvor er...? (Danish, Norwegian), Hvar er...? (Icelandic), Missä on...? (Finnish)

9. I would like...: Jag skulle vilja... (Swedish), Jeg vil gerne... (Danish), Jeg vil gjerne... (Norwegian), Ég vil... (Icelandic), Haluaisin... (Finnish)

10. Can you help me?: Kan du hjälpa mig? (Swedish), Kan du hjælpe mig? (Danish), Kan du hjelpe meg? (Norwegian), Getur þú hjálpað mér? (Icelandic), Voitko auttaa minua? (Finnish)

11. How much is it?: Hur mycket kostar det? (Swedish), Hvad koster det? (Danish), Hva koster det? (Norwegian), Hvað kostar það? (Icelandic), Paljonko se maksaa? (Finnish)

12. I don't understand: Jag förstår inte (Swedish), Jeg forstår ikke (Danish, Norwegian), Ég skil ekki (Icelandic), En ymmärrä (Finnish)

13. Cheers!: Skål! (Swedish, Danish, Norwegian), Skál! (Icelandic), Kippis! (Finnish)

Cash At The Airport Is Expensive

For tourists visiting Scandinavia, it's important to be aware that cash at the airport can be expensive. While using a credit card or ATM is often the most convenient and safe way to obtain local currency, there are additional fees and charges that can add up quickly, particularly when using cash at the airport. In this guide, we will discuss the reasons why cash at the airport is expensive in Scandinavia, and some alternative options for obtaining local currency.

Reasons Why Cash at the Airport is Expensive

There are several reasons why cash at the airport is expensive in Scandinavia, including:

- **Exchange rates:** Exchange rates at the airport are often much higher than those offered by banks and exchange bureaus in the city. This is because airports charge higher fees to exchange money due to their location and convenience.

- **Fees and commissions:** In addition to exchange rates, airports also charge additional fees and commissions for exchanging money. This can include handling fees, commissions, and other surcharges that can quickly add up.

- **Limited options:** At the airport, there may be limited options for exchanging money, which can result in a lack of competition and higher prices.

Alternative Options for Obtaining Local Currency

To avoid the high fees associated with cash at the airport, there are several alternative options for obtaining local currency in Scandinavia, including:

- **Credit cards:** Using a credit card for purchases and cash withdrawals can often be a more cost-effective option. However, it's important to check with your credit card company beforehand to ensure that they do not charge additional fees for foreign transactions.

- **ATM machines:** Using an ATM machine to withdraw local currency is another convenient and cost-effective option. However, it's important to check with your bank beforehand to ensure that they do not charge additional fees for foreign transactions.

- **Exchange bureaus:** Exchange bureaus are often found in major cities and offer competitive exchange rates and lower fees than those found at airports. It's important to compare rates and fees from different bureaus to ensure that you get the best deal.

- **Local banks:** Local banks can also offer competitive exchange rates and lower fees than those found at airports. It's important to check with your bank beforehand to ensure that they do not charge additional fees for foreign transactions.

Tips for Saving Money on Currency Exchange

To save money on currency exchange, consider the following tips:

- **Plan ahead:** Before you travel, research the exchange rates and fees for different currency exchange options. This will help you to make an informed decision and avoid unnecessary fees.

- **Avoid exchanging money at the airport:** While it may be convenient, exchanging money at the airport is often the most expensive option. Consider using a credit card, ATM, exchange bureau, or local bank instead.

- **Use a credit card with no foreign transaction fees:** If you plan to use a credit card for purchases and cash withdrawals, consider using one that does not charge foreign transaction fees.

- **Withdraw larger amounts of cash:** When using an ATM machine, withdrawing larger amounts of cash can help to reduce the number of transactions and associated fees.

- **Be aware of hidden fees:** When using a credit card or ATM, be aware of hidden fees and charges, such as ATM surcharges or currency conversion fees.

CONCLUSION

Tips For Solo Travelers, Families, And LGBTQ+ Travelers

Tips for Solo Travelers:

- Safety is not a big issue in Scandinavia, but it's always better to take precautions. Stay in well-lit areas and avoid empty streets at night.

- Solo travelers can save money by staying in hostels or budget hotels. Scandinavia has a good network of hostels that are safe, clean, and affordable.

- Use public transport to save money on travel. Scandinavia has a reliable public transport system, including buses, trains, and metros.

- Don't be afraid to strike up a conversation with locals. Scandinavians are known to be friendly and open to visitors.

- Research cultural and historical landmarks in advance and book in advance to avoid last-minute disappointments.

Tips for Families:

- Scandinavia is known for its family-friendly atmosphere. Many attractions offer discounts for families.
- Theme parks and adventure parks are great for kids. There are many options in Scandinavia, including Tivoli Gardens in Copenhagen, Liseberg in Gothenburg, and Tusenfryd in Oslo.
- Visit museums and zoos. Scandinavian museums and zoos are engaging and interactive, making them ideal for families with children.
- Bring warm clothing. Scandinavia can get cold, even in summer. Be sure to pack warm jackets, hats, and gloves.
- Try local cuisine. Scandinavian food is delicious and there are plenty of family-friendly restaurants to choose from.

Tips for LGBTQ+ Travelers:

- Scandinavia is generally considered a safe destination for LGBTQ+ travelers, with a high level of acceptance and equality.
- Pride festivals are held in many cities across Scandinavia. Attending a Pride festival is a great way to meet local LGBTQ+ communities.

- Many bars and clubs in Scandinavia are LGBTQ+ friendly. Check out local listings to find bars and clubs that are specifically LGBTQ+ oriented.

- Be aware of the laws and customs of the country you are visiting. Some countries in Scandinavia may have different laws and customs regarding LGBTQ+ issues.

- Use common sense and exercise caution when traveling to unfamiliar areas, just as you would anywhere else in the world.

- Some cities in Scandinavia are more LGBTQ+ friendly than others. For example, Copenhagen is known for being one of the most LGBTQ+ friendly cities in the world.

- Many hotels and accommodations in Scandinavia are LGBTQ+ friendly. Look for accommodations that have a reputation for being inclusive and welcoming.

- LGBTQ+ travelers should also consider attending cultural events, such as art exhibitions or concerts, to experience local culture and meet like-minded people.

- Research LGBTQ+ organizations or groups in the area you are visiting. Many organizations host social events, community meetings, or cultural gatherings.

- Finally, remember to be respectful of local customs and traditions, and follow local laws and regulations. This will help ensure a safe and enjoyable trip for LGBTQ+ travelers in Scandinavia.

Additional Resources and Contact Information

Here are some additional resources and contact information for tourists in Scandinavia:

- **Visit Scandinavia:** The official tourism website for Scandinavia, which provides information on travel, accommodations, attractions, and events in Denmark, Norway, and Sweden.

Website: https://www.visitscandinavia.com/

- **Visit Denmark:** The official tourism website for Denmark, which provides information on travel, accommodations, attractions, and events in Denmark.

Website: https://www.visitdenmark.com/

- **Visit Norway:** The official tourism website for Norway, which provides information on travel, accommodations, attractions, and events in Norway.

Website: https://www.visitnorway.com/

- **Visit Sweden:** The official tourism website for Sweden, which provides information on travel, accommodations, attractions, and events in Sweden.

Website: https://visitsweden.com/

- **Scandinavia Tourist Board:** A network of tourism organizations in Denmark, Norway, and Sweden, which provides information on travel, accommodations, attractions, and events in Scandinavia.

Website: https://scandinaviantravel.com/

- **Emergency Services:** In case of emergency, dial 112 from any phone in Scandinavia to reach emergency services.